ABC Television Rich Walcoff...

"I've used the tools in this book every day since I read it. Even with my kids. What's amazing is that this information just isn't available anywhere else. This is an extraordinary book. I couldn't put it down."

NBC Radio Network News Bob Fuss...

"Forget everything you think you know about how to win friends and influence people and read this book! Dr. David Stiebel stands conventional wisdom on its head with a better approach that is fresh and really works."

CBS News Claudia Marshall...

"Dr. David Stiebel's techniques are brilliant because they're simple. And he has written about them with such clarity and FUN as to make dealing with problems almost ENJOYABLE."

National Public Radio Lynne Terry...

"When Talking Makes Things *Worse!* is a gem. Extremely readable and down-to-earth, this book offers a smart, practical strategy on how to change our lives and everyone else's—for the better."

Dave Barry Pulitzer Prize-winning humorist...

"This is an excellent book. Or at least the part about worm sex is."

When
talking
makes things
WORSE!

Dr. David Stiebel (pronounced "Steeble")
CBS, NBC, ABC News, National Public Radio, Canadian Broadcasting Corporation, Associated Press, United Press International, and CNN have tapped him as an on-air analyst and correspondent. The press has called him "an acknowledged wizard at settling feuds," "a master of mediation"—a world-renowned negotiation adviser to corporate and government leaders.

Dr. David Stiebel has consulted to Fortune 500 companies such as Lockheed and Xerox, in addition to teaching at the University of California, Berkeley and guest lecturing at 14 other universities. He is a popular convention speaker.

According to a UCLA study, *managers who took Dr. Stiebel's course scored 98% higher in negotiation skills than their colleagues.*

David Horsey (illustrator)
The award-winning nationally syndicated editorial cartoonist and columnist is featured regularly in America's top business magazines and newspapers. His credits include *The New York Times, The Washington Post, Los Angeles Times, Newsweek, Business Week,* and *Fortune.* His cartoons are syndicated to more than 300 newspapers and appear daily in the *Seattle Post-Intelligencer.*

A Rotary Foundation scholar, David Horsey earned his MA in International Relations from the University of Kent at Canterbury in England. He was born in Evansville, Indiana.

When
talking
makes things
WORSE!

Resolving problems
when communication fails

Dr. David Stiebel

Illustrated by David Horsey

WHITEHALL
&
NOLTON

This book is available at quantity discounts, both in hardcover and in a four-cassette audio format. The audio version includes recordings of actual negotiations, with analysis from the author and the participants themselves. Visit your local bookseller or write to Whitehall & Nolton, 5120 Northaven, Dallas, TX 75229-4353.

Important legal disclaimer: This book does not reprint all information on the subject; rather, this book supplements, complements, or amplifies other works. You are urged to read all the available material. (Continued on page 269.)

LIBRARY OF CONGRESS CATALOGING-IN-PUBLICATION DATA

Stiebel, David.
When talking makes things worse!: resolving problems when communication fails / David Stiebel; illustrated by David Horsey.
p. cm.
Includes index.
ISBN 1-888430-42-7
1. Negotiation. 2. Interpersonal communication. I. Title.
BF637.N4S75 1997
158'.5—dc20 96-23674 CIP

Manufactured in the United States of America. Distributed to the trade by Andrews and McMeel, 4520 Main Street, Kansas City, MO 64111.

To Naomi, Alice, Rich, Fay, and Jonathan

Contents

Thinking on your feet

Here's how to use the four strategic steps under pressure.

221

When
talking
makes things
WORSE!

PREFACE

"What we've got here is a failure to communicate."

So many people have repeated that platitude for so long, it's become so ingrained in our way of thinking, that we actually believe it. We believe that if only we could understand each other better, our problems would go away. Problems at home and at work. Problems with a marriage or with a merger.

How ironic.

Because that cliché was never true to begin with.

It's from the movie *Cool Hand Luke*. A prison inmate played by Paul Newman has tried to escape from his chain gang. As punishment his legs are put in chains, in front of all the other prisoners. The captain of the gang looks at those chains and says, "They're going to remind you of what I've been saying, for your own good."

Paul Newman replies, "Wish you'd stop being so good to me, captain."

The captain seethes, "Don't you *ever* talk that way to me." And he takes his blackjack and strikes Paul Newman so hard, Newman goes tumbling down a slope. The captain, played by Strother Martin, explains to the other members of the chain gang: "What we've got here...is a failure to communicate!"

Yeah, right.

They understand each other. They understand that

each of them is set on doing what he wants to do. They understand that they are locked in a test of wills. Paul Newman runs away again. And the captain beats him again. And again. And again. And threatens to kill Paul Newman if he runs away a third time. And so Paul Newman does.

And this is when the famous line appears in the movie for the last time. Paul Newman, trapped in a barn, opens the door, looks at the officers surrounding the place, half laughs to himself; then he grins and shouts toward the captain..."Now what we got here...is a failure to communicate!" A rifle bullet rips through him and he is dead.

A failure to communicate?

Communication is not the problem here, any more than it's the problem in a wide range of disagreements in everyday life.

Yet that statement—"What we've got here is a failure to communicate"—has stuck with us and become an aphorism. It's become conventional wisdom. We have taken a movie line that was never intended to be taken at face value and we have applied it seriously to problems in the real world.

What we *really* have here is a lot of talk that makes things worse.

This book is dedicated to exploding the conventional wisdom that "what we've got here is a failure to communicate." It provides a better approach to solving problems.

OVERVIEW

Don't just keep talking!

W e all know that the key to getting along with people and working things out is communication... right?

We say, "Why don't we talk it out."

We think, "As long as we're talking, there's hope."

It doesn't matter if the problem is with your spouse, your boss, your client, your landlord, your co-worker, or your child. People believe that if you listen and explain things openly and honestly, *any* problem will be solved.

Don't count on it.

Expressing your true feelings, honest opinions, and underlying interests does not always bring people closer together. Often, quite the opposite. Better understanding can drive you further apart.

What determines whether talking will succeed or backfire?

Strategy.

And that's what this book is all about.

How to think strategically on your feet

Simply put, a strategy is an approach to help you achieve your goal. There are all kinds of strategies—effective and ineffective, manipulative and cooperative.

This book is *not* about how to design a manipulative or exploitative strategy for selfish gain. This book is

15

about how to develop a strategy that persuades someone to cooperate with you and solve a problem.

You might think of strategy as requiring a long time
to prepare. Often, you don't have time. You've got
ten minutes before a big meeting. Or you've got to
think strategically on the spur of the moment. In the
real world, you've got to figure out the right thing to
do *right now* to get what you want.

This book will help you do that. It will show you a
simple, systematic way to think strategically. By practicing the method in this book, you can not only develop a game plan in advance; you can train yourself to
think on your feet to get someone to budge.

It is a challenge to think strategically amidst frustration and confusion. Often, ideas flood into your head
only after the discussion. Hours later you think, "I
wish I had said that! If only I had thought of it at the
time!"

A few individuals always seem to know the right
thing to do to turn a situation around and defuse a
confrontation. It's quite a skill.

And like any skill, it can be learned.

The four strategic steps

This book introduces the method of *strategic communication*. Strategic communication helps you examine a
situation quickly to decide what to do. The method
helps you develop an approach to working things out,
based on the specific situation you're dealing with.

In any situation, you've got to attend to four fundamental strategic elements: the problem, the goal, the method, and the result. Each step of strategic communication focuses on one of these elements and suggests how to deal with it.

1. The problem: *Decide whether you have a misunderstanding or a true disagreement.*
2. The goal: *Create the other person's next move.*
3. The method: *Use their own perceptions to convince them.*
4. The result: *Predict the other person's response.*

These four strategic steps help you avoid common hidden pitfalls in which communication backfires.

Strategic step #1: Decide whether you have a misunderstanding or a true disagreement. This step steers you clear of a big trap—plunging in to resolve *the wrong problem.*

A *misunderstanding* is a failure to understand each other accurately. A *true disagreement* is a failure to agree that would persist despite the most accurate understanding.

In a misunderstanding, the solution is simple: you understand each other accurately, the problem disappears. In a true disagreement, you need a strategy to persuade them.

There are many books on coping with misunderstandings. This book focuses on using strategy to handle *true disagreements.*

Strategic step #2: Create the other person's next move. Suppose you're in a true disagreement with

Sally, your longtime friend and business partner, over whether she should repay the $5,000 you loaned her.

The first question you might ask yourself is, "What should I do?" But to influence her, ask yourself instead: "What do I want *her* to do?"

Many negotiation books suggest you push Sally to her *bottom line*—the most she could do for you *ultimately*. It's much more useful to focus on her *immediate limit*—the most that Sally is willing and able to do for you *right now*.

Ultimately, she might give you the whole $5,000. But now? Perhaps the most that Sally will do is to agree to review her finances and meet again. To reach an ultimate settlement, lead the other person to take one realistic action after another.

Strategic step #3: Use their own perceptions to convince them. To persuade Sally, you've got to explain why she's wrong and should do what you want instead. You'll have to overcome her attitudes and beliefs...right?

Wrong. That's going about it the hard way.

Rather than fighting her perceptions, make her perceptions the very foundation of your approach. *People find their own perceptions the most convincing.* Whether you're playing tough or nice, start from *her* perspective and, tactfully, use her own perceptions to lead her to make the move you want.

Strategic step #4: Predict the other person's response. It's easy to get emotionally ensnared in an argument, but many emotional traps are foreseeable.

To sidestep a trap before things escalate, you've got to anticipate how Sally is *likely* to respond to your next move. A major mistake is to focus on what you *want* her to do.

This book offers a method to predict someone's response correctly. Then you can decide whether to proceed with your intended approach or devise another one instead.

Which will help you more?

Conventional wisdom:	Strategic communication:
Listen and explain, and *any* problem can be solved.	Decide whether you have a misunderstanding or a true disagreement.
Decide what *you* should do to get what you want.	Create the other person's next move.
Explain why they're wrong and refute their beliefs.	Use their own perceptions to convince them.
Once you figure out what to do, *just do it!*	Predict the other person's response.

How this book is organized

The next chapter, *The Great Myth of Hidden Harmony,* reveals how the approach of improving understanding makes problems worse. Then we delve into the alternate approach—the method of strategic communication. There are four chapters explaining how to use the four steps. Each chapter focuses on one step and gives real-life examples.

As you start using strategic communication, you're bound to have questions. And so, there is a chapter that provides answers.

The final chapter shows all four strategic steps in action together. You'll observe how to use them to plan rapidly before an interaction. You'll see the strategic steps applied on the spur of the moment, and I'll explain the rationale behind each move.

At the end of each chapter, you'll find a summary of key points for applying the ideas you've just read.

What if they use this method, too?

You should be so lucky. I *hope* that you are fortunate enough to deal with someone who is thinking constructively about how to solve the problem with you. All too often, the other person is not. They are consumed by their own emotions and lashing out, at times trying to control or trick you.

How can you succeed if the other person is also using strategic communication? The answer is: Much more easily. If you are both systematically focused on working things out, you'll make progress faster.

This book is designed to help you deal with even the toughest people problems, when someone stubbornly digs in and refuses to budge at all. However, if the other person is willing to cooperate and think strategically, so much the better.

Give them a copy of this book.

Even if you're enemies?

Especially if you're enemies. It will be easier to resolve the problem if you aren't the only one trying. By introducing the other side to strategic communication, you'll be reducing the risk of stalemate.

No matter whether they're willing to cooperate, go ahead and use strategic communication yourself. You can use this method regardless of whether they do.

Strategic communication is battle-tested

The method in this book has evolved from my work as a negotiation adviser with corporate and government officials and also from work with my students at the University of California, Berkeley. Together, we have used strategic communication to resolve a wide range of personal and professional issues with spouses, bosses, bureaucrats, neighbors, employees, landlords, tenants, customers, drug dealers, ex-cons, and teenagers.

The principles you'll read about have been tested over the years with thousands of individuals, including department heads, senior managers, foreign executives, lawyers, children, federal government officials, state and local politicians, judges, labor negotiators, insurance adjusters, salespeople, and small-business owners in industries ranging from financial services to transportation.

Strategic communication can be used by a chief executive to resolve a corporate takeover battle, by a mediator to avert a strike, by a police officer to defuse a confrontation, and by a couple to settle an argument about where to go out for dinner.

Anyone can use this method.

WHY THINGS GET WORSE

The Great Myth of Hidden Harmony

*We've all been
in situations where
we talk and talk—
and succeed only
in banging heads
with the other person.
Communication,
the very tool that's
supposed to make
things better, not only
lets us down but often
makes things WORSE.
This chapter
explains why.*

Not many people are accustomed to behaving strategically. Look at this statistic from a study by the National Institute for Dispute Resolution:

2%.

That's how many Americans say they actually *think* before responding in an argument. No wonder talking makes things worse. We're charging in with no better plan than to speak our mind.

Why do we do this?

We may not realize it, but many Americans rely on a fundamental belief, which I call the Great Myth of Hidden Harmony: *Deep down, we all agree. People just need to understand each other better.* The assumption is: *There is no conflict, only poor understanding.*

This view of human nature is appealing because it is so optimistic: A stubborn person is merely unenlightened, so there is hope! You get the person to see the light, and it will be possible to work things out.

No doubt you have seen situations where this is true. But the Great Myth of Hidden Harmony overgeneralizes. It suggests two steps to make *any* problem disappear:

1. *Listen with an open mind.* In some cases, this is downright ludicrous. My favorite example is a friend of mine who actually said: "I'm sure there is a logical reason my boyfriend has not called me for five weeks. Once I understand it, I have faith our relationship will be fine." (It wasn't.)

2. *Explain yourself clearly.* This advice, too, is not always helpful. Imagine how you'd feel if your boss explained clearly to you: "I know you've worked here five years and that Linda's brand new. I'm giving her the promotion instead of you because her work is better. Now that you understand...I trust you have no hard feelings. Right?" Wrong.

The Great Myth of Hidden Harmony has generated three rules of thumb. People who disagree should:

- discuss their honest opinions,
- explore their true interests, and
- reveal their sincere feelings.

These sound reasonable. Certainly it's good to be honest. And if we express our underlying goals, we'll see how much we have in common. And if we discuss and respect each other's real feelings, any problem should go away, right?

Let's take a look.

Discussing honest opinions

We think it's good to "be candid," to "get it out in the open." We admire "straight talk." People believe that honesty makes for better human relations. For example, if only others could tell us their honest opinions about us, we could change and get along better. Unfortunately...

Often, the more you honestly understand each other, the more you grow to *dislike* each other. All the sales employees at a company in California met for

a weekend retreat to share their honest opinions about what they were each doing well and how they could each improve, both personally and professionally. This would boost team performance and shore up sales.

That was the theory.

Here are a few of the comments that actually came out during this retreat:

"You really look good with a few extra pounds! Really, I mean it! You look great!"

"You're always talking on the phone about your emotional problems. Have you thought about seeing a psychologist?"

"Perhaps you wouldn't have so much trouble with your skin if you wore less makeup!"

Do you think this candid exchange of views fostered harmony and bolstered sales? You're right: it didn't. The first month after this weekend retreat, sales *dropped* 12%.

Poor understanding was not the problem here. Everyone was communicating clearly. The problem was that people understood each other all too well.

Revealing your underlying interests

If we believe in the magic of understanding, we reveal our true goals and discover—voila!—they are compatible.

I'm skeptical about this. Take a typical problem at work: your boss wants you to spend evenings putting in free overtime; you prefer not to. So you meet to discuss your true goals: your boss would like her project completed on schedule; you wish to go home and watch TV.

Oops!

Underlying interests are not always compatible. Here, revealing your true goal won't resolve anything. All it will do is to trigger a slight increase in the unemployment rate.

Discussing your motivations can make things worse. Here are three reasons why:

1. Disclosing your interests can tempt an opponent to exploit you. Let's say you are shopping for a house. Your spouse walks into one house with you and exclaims, "It's got everything we've been looking for— a fireplace, skylights, even a cottage in back for Grandma!" Now the sellers know you really want what they've got. Will they compromise on the price?

Not if they're playing hardball. They might even raise the price ("We underestimated the market for this property.")

2. If you divulge your objective, the person may compete with you to achieve it. Back at work, you develop a new production method that's 50% faster. It's sure to impress the division manager, and you know you'll get a promotion. You might even get your boss' job.

Your boss seems eager to adopt your new method until you let slip your underlying interest, "And the division manager will love it!"

Suddenly your boss falls silent. She needs time to think it over.

That afternoon, the division manager holds a meeting applauding a new production method that's 50% faster, developed by...your boss.

That's when you realize: sometimes it's better to keep your mouth shut. Until you mentioned your interest in impressing the division head, your boss hadn't thought of stealing credit.

3. Your real goal may antagonize the other side. Take the experience of Mr. Chandra, who had recently arrived in America as an immigrant. He had been trained as a librarian in his native country, and he got a job interview at a library here.

Unfortunately, Mr. Chandra did not know the way Americans are expected to behave in job interviews.

The interviewer asked, "Why do you want to work *here?*" Of course, most American applicants know that we are expected to care enough about the organization to have done research about it, so that during the interview we can lie and explain why this job is a perfect match for us.

Mr. Chandra did not know he was supposed to do anything like this, so he simply revealed his underlying interest. He said, "Oh, I don't care about working *here.* I just need a job."

"At any library?" The interviewer wanted to give Mr. Chandra a chance to rehabilitate himself.

Mr. Chandra made things worse by clarifying his true interest: "Sure, any library will do."

As you probably guessed, Mr. Chandra did not get this job.

Expressing your true feelings

For decades, psychologists have told us, "Don't push down your feelings." This has given rise to the popular notion that to cultivate a solid relationship, you should always express your true feelings.

Think twice about that.

Your true feelings may hurt or offend the other person. I personally learned this my first year in college. As you will soon see, I was not what you'd call socially "smooth" with women. For reasons that are still unclear to me, an extremely attractive co-ed named Jennifer, whom I'd had a crush on all semester, decided to go out with me. Our relationship went very well until she became concerned that I liked her solely for her looks. She raised the issue one night when we were cuddled up together in front of the fireplace.

She said, "I think you're going out with me because I'm blonde." I wanted to set her straight. I said, "Absolutely not true! Fact is, I'm really not especially attracted to blondes."

I spent the next two hours trying to explain that particular true feeling of mine.

But it did not take me that long to realize I had made a *major* mistake by expressing it. That realization came almost immediately—when Jennifer pulled away, looked at me in disbelief, and stammered out, "You mean...you don't find me attractive??"

"No, no, no, that's not true!" I was trying to allay her concerns, so I reclarified my feelings: "You're *very* attractive! I'm just more attracted to brunettes, so naturally I wouldn't be going out with you solely for your looks."

Jennifer wanted to get this straight. "OK, so you— you like me, you just find other women more *appealing* than me?" This clarifying question tightened the noose I had looped around my own neck. Things went downhill from there.

I was a man in desperate need of a strategy. I knew Jennifer was asking for reassurance. I could have told her what I liked about her personality. *That's* what she wanted me to tell her, not that I was naturally more attracted to brunettes. (She explained all this to me, as she was breaking up with me.)

As my experience with Jennifer points out rather painfully, *expressing your true feelings can make things worse.* My clear communication only created a new argument over whether I was attracted to her.

Expressing your true feelings can be insensitive. You may assume that the other person wants to know every true feeling you have, even if it does hurt or offend them. If that is your assumption, check it out with them. Many people would prefer that you kept some true feelings to yourself.

In Jennifer's own words—which I still remember: "Even if you are more attracted to brunettes, I would think you'd have the decency not to *tell* me!"

Why can't we say what we want?

Why can't we come out and say what's on our minds, and then reach a solution that satisfies everyone?

I wish it were always that easy. That's part of the appeal of the Great Myth of Hidden Harmony. It makes problems seem so...*simple* to resolve.

There are times when you may wish to speak out regardless of the consequences, to vent anger or frustration.

But if you care how the other person responds, if your purpose is to win them over, then that requires persuasion. You can disregard strategy and charge in recklessly, but that is no recipe for good results.

Be clear on your purpose: is it self-expression or persuasion? Don't fool yourself that uncensored self-expression is a wise standard procedure for resolving problems.

Does talking more always help?

Conventional wisdom says yes:	Strategic communication says no:
The key to working things out is communication.	Talking *can* backfire. The key to success is strategy.
The way to settle differences is to speak your mind.	*Think* before responding in an argument.
It always helps to understand each other better.	Better understanding can drive people further apart.
If we understand each other, we will agree.	We may understand each other yet *still* disagree.
When no one will budge, the answer is to talk more.	Before talking makes things worse, develop a sound strategy.

There is no universal strategy

If it is not a good standard approach to blurt out whatever is on your mind, then what *is* the universal strategy for settling differences?

There is none.

There is no single strategy that will persuade anyone, anytime to resolve any problem you may have.

Some scholars in dispute resolution have spent years looking for a universal strategy. But a stock strategy, such as improving understanding, that succeeds in one case can do major damage in another.

No single formula can resolve all issues, just as no single pill can cure all diseases.

There is, however, a series of steps you can use to *develop* a strategy that will succeed in your specific case.

That's what this book is about.

Don't rely on a stock technique. You may think, "If it's worked before, it will work again." Not necessarily. After one of my conference presentations, an executive came up to me and asked, "Whenever a client is upset, I offer to split the difference. It's worked many times. But I've always wondered: Is it a good idea?"

Not as a universal strategy, no. Offering to split the difference can work in many cases and still be a bad idea in *this particular* case. I've seen the other person reply, "I'm sorry, I can't split the difference with you. But we're very close now. If only you can bridge the small remaining gap, we'll have a deal."

What's wrong with offering to split the difference

and hoping that it will work? The risk is that, as in this case, not only do you fail to settle anything, you ensure that the eventual terms will be worse for you.

Regardless of how many times a given strategy has succeeded in the past, you've got to examine the present situation anew. And you can, using the four strategic steps in this book.

Develop a plan suited to the situation

Many of us have only a few strategies for dealing with differences. In a new situation, we instinctively apply one of those familiar strategies.

That's a big mistake. Listen to the advice of General George Patton. "One does not [take a strategic] plan and then try to make the circumstances fit those plans," he said. "One tries to make [strategic] plans fit the circumstances. I think the difference between success and failure in high command depends on the ability, or the lack of it, to do just that."

Don't start with a stock strategy and try to impose it on the situation. Instead, look at the situation and develop a strategy that fits it. Thinking strategically requires that you develop an approach that will work in *your* specific situation.

There is a method you can use to help you do that. A method that enables you to size up your situation quickly and design a strategy based on the particular circumstances you face.

That method is strategic communication.

❖ *Key points for applying ideas in:*
The Great Myth of Hidden Harmony

1. Recognize that better understanding cannot resolve
    all problems. Better understanding can drive peo-
    ple further apart. Often the more you understand
    each other, the more you *dislike* each other.

2. Think carefully before revealing your true goal.
    You may be hoping that it will be compatible with
    the other side's objective. But beware of three
    traps:
    *   Revealing your goal can tempt an opponent to
        exploit you.
    *   The other person may compete with you to
        achieve your objective.
    *   Your objective may antagonize the other side.

3. When you're tempted to blurt out what's on your
    mind, remember your purpose: is it self-expression
    or persuasion? Uncensored self-expression is hardly
    a wise standard procedure for resolving problems.

4. Create a strategy that is appropriate to *your specific
    situation.* A stock strategy (such as improving un-
    derstanding) that succeeds in one case can do major
    damage in another.

THE SOLUTION:
The Four Steps
of Strategic Communication

Decide whether you have a misunderstanding or a true disagreement

Often, poor communication is not the cause of the problem. So if you keep trying to understand each other better, you will not resolve the problem—and you may worsen it. Before plunging in, you need to identify the REAL problem you are facing. This chapter provides a simple test to do just that.

If you work at a major corporation that personally cares very deeply about you as an individual, chances are it has an open-door policy. This means that even the lowliest worker can air a complaint to Senior Management. Senior Management will listen to you and resolve the issue satisfactorily. You need not fear reprisal. Rest assured, with an open-door policy, Senior Management is committed to open, two-way communication.

At least in theory.

A gap between theory and practice allegedly appeared at a rocket manufacturer in southern California. The story illustrates the flawed approach that many of us take when we try to resolve problems—the approach of assuming that the other person needs only to understand us better. The story appeared in one of America's major newspapers. I cannot comment on the truth or lack of truth of the article; I can tell you only what the newspaper reported:

Workers were being laid off, and allegedly, most of those remaining were told they would not get raises; instead, they'd get one-time bonuses. And so an engineer named Tom Shackleberry decided to write the company's president.

He wrote that Senior Management was doing "little to inspire confidence" among workers. He complained that most workers were being told to sacrifice their pay raises even though, he said, the company had

43

just reported a 10% increase in profits and even though, he said, Senior Management was continuing to give itself increases up to 22%.

He said, "Your calls for other employees to sacrifice...ring especially hollow." He called the decision about raises "one of the worst examples of arrogant, short-sighted, self-serving management that I have ever seen."

Mr. Shackleberry continued: "For top management to claim that they are trying to reduce overhead costs . . . while their own compensation skyrockets is *abhorrent and unethical.*"

By now you are wondering just how open that "open door" really was. Shackleberry found out when he got a reply from the Vice President for Human Resources, whom I will refer to as Virgil W. Grimm.

Mr. Grimm wrote: "Most of the premises and assumptions on which you base your attacks are wrong."

He went on: "I suggest that you have a calm discussion with your management as to what the Company is doing and the rationale for it. If, after getting a full explanation of the facts and circumstances, you still feel like writing about the 'abhorrent and unethical' behavior of the Company's leadership, you probably will feel better doing so from a position at an employer more in keeping with your theories."

Shackleberry comments, "It didn't take a rocket scientist to see what the real message was—and I *am* a rocket scientist."

He was so taken aback by what the newspaper calls

the "implied threat" that he "shared copies of the two letters with a few friends. Those friends sent copies to a few of their friends.

"And so on.

"And on.

"Soon, the two letters were zipping by fax" throughout the corporation's southern California offices—which employed 17,300 people—and even reached the company's facilities in Texas and Florida. Shackleberry says the faxes also got to employees in England and Australia.

There was so much controversy throughout the organization that the company president, whom I will refer to as Filbert T. Witherspoon III, finally commented personally in a company newsletter.

Witherspoon acknowledged that "a response written to one employee's letter gave rise to concerns about the reality of open, two-way communication." Since his employees did not seem to understand the reality, Mr. Witherspoon clarified it: "Let me emphasize that I intend to continue my policy of open communication." Finally, he did meet with Shackleberry.

Do you think he apologized even for the tone of the VP's letter?

According to the newspaper, he did not.

But then, why should he? There was no problem with Senior Management, was there? Senior Management was *misunderstood*—first by Shackleberry, then by other employees. Shackleberry needed to get a "full explanation." The employees had to get clarification.

Witherspoon was acting according to the Great Myth of Hidden Harmony: If only we understand each other, we'll agree. His twist on it was: If only you understand *me,* we'll agree.

If this approach strikes you as patronizing and self-centered, it should also strike you as familiar.

Because this is the approach many of us take when we get into an argument.

The "We Can Work It Out" approach

John Lennon and Paul McCartney are the authors of "We Can Work It Out." As any Beatles fan knows, it's a song about how to resolve problems by improving understanding.

But not the way you might think.

If you listen carefully to the lyrics, you realize that Lennon and McCartney's idea of "working it out" is the same as Witherspoon's. "Working it out" means "see it *my* way."

> *Try to see it my way.*
> *Do I have to keep on talking 'till I can't go on?*
> *While you see it your way,*
> *There's a chance that we might fall apart before*
>   *too long.*
> *We can work it out,*
> *We can work it out.*

Intentionally or not, these lyrics very accurately describe the way many people deal with a difference of opinion. They each start with the assumption that they are right; then they push their point of view, determined to get their way, convinced that they can get the other side to give in.

They know, after all, that they are logically correct.

The power of logic

Many people believe in resolving their differences in a logical and orderly manner: I state my position with supporting facts, you do the same, we point out the errors in each other's reasoning, and the most logical view will prevail. It's all very sensible.

This approach can work if everyone's engaged in a joint search for truth, rationally and dispassionately, with no egos or interests at stake. If you are dealing with people who are this selfless, you are probably not reading this book and you probably live on a different planet.

How do *normal* human beings respond to a new idea? They compare it to what they already believe. If the new idea fits their established views, they accept it. If not, they reject it.

Does this behavior sound unreasonable? It is. It's also human nature. It explains why people see only the strengths of their argument and only the weaknesses of the other side's. *People literally want to see the world their way.* Humans believed that the sun revolved around the earth. Do you know how long it took our species to admit we were wrong?

Centuries! That's a testimony to how stubborn we are as a life form and how much we resist change.

Lest you think we've evolved since then, try an experiment. Clip a provocative commentary from the editorial page of your local newspaper. Show it to two people on opposite sides of the issue—say, a liberal and a conservative.

Then ask them if it changed their minds.

Time after time, the liberal finds facts in the clipping that support the liberal perspective; the conservative finds facts that confirm the conservative position. They do not change their minds at all.

Which view of human nature is more realistic?

Conventional wisdom:	Strategic communication:
People care about learning the objective truth.	People care about proving they are right.
Human beings are capable of seeing things dispassionately.	Human beings prefer to see the world their way.
People change their minds if you show them the facts.	People interpret the facts to support their beliefs.
People are reasonable and will admit when you're right.	People react emotionally and will defend their position.

Trying to change people's minds is one of the hardest ways to resolve an argument. They have to abandon their beliefs to accept yours. That's the reverse of what people commonly do. In general, *people prefer to reinterpret the facts to suit their preconceptions rather than to admit they're wrong.*

As a rule, when people feel under attack, they react emotionally. They figure, "Uh-oh, I'd better shore up my position." They defend themselves and attack the other side. Newton's law: For every action there is an equal and opposite reaction. If one person pushes, the other wants to shove back.

The Talking Trap

Take, for instance, the stereotypical argument between husband and wife over where to go on vacation. Look what happens if they each keep pushing, trying to explain why they're right. The frustration of talking in circles escalates into deadlock, as they follow the four trademark steps of the Talking Trap:

1. I make a demand, you make a demand.

He says, "Honey, I've got it! For our vacation this year, we are going to drive to the sites of all the major Civil War battles!"

She says, "Oh, no, not that again! I will not be stuck in a hot car day after day. For our vacation, we are going to Florida to vegetate in the sun!"

2. I explain my position, you explain yours.

He says, "But you know how much I love the Civil War!"

She says, "But you know how much I love lying on the beach doing absolutely nothing!"

3. I announce I'm digging in, you do the same.
He says, "Look, we're going to the Civil War sites,
        and I don't want to argue about it."
She says, "No, *you're* going on your Civil War trek.
        I'm sipping piña coladas in Florida."

4. I stop talking, you stop talking.
He picks up the mail and refuses to look at her.
She turns up the radio and tunes him out.

Classic example of the Talking Trap. So is Dr. Seuss' tale of the Zax. A North-Going Zax bumps into a South-Going Zax. They each demand that the other get out of the way (that's step one of the Talking Trap). They proceed to explain their positions (step two). Then, predictably, they dig in (step three):

> *Then the North-Going Zax puffed his chest up*
>   *with pride.*
> *"I never," he said, "take a step to one side.*
> *And I'll prove to you that I won't change my ways*
> *If I have to keep standing here fifty-nine days!"*

Sure enough, communication breaks down (step four), each Zax with its hands on its hips, refusing to budge.

When people aren't talking, we assume that they must not understand each other and that they need to listen and explain things openly and honestly. (Again, we're relying on the Great Myth of Hidden Harmony: If only they understood each other, they'd agree.)

But in the Talking Trap, people (and also Zax) stop talking because they *do* understand. They *know* they disagree.

This was the case when a teachers' union broke off contract talks. They understood the school district's pay offer; they wanted to protest it by breaking off talks. Poor communication was not the *cause* of this problem.

It was the *result.*

In a true disagreement, there's often plenty of understanding. *More* understanding could not resolve the teachers' pay dispute. In fact, when people are stuck in the Talking Trap, going 'round and 'round explaining themselves, trying harder only makes things *worse.*

It does no good to do the same wrong thing with more intensity.

When is greater understanding the answer?

More understanding will help only if lack of understanding is the problem. You need to know what you're dealing with—a misunderstanding or a true disagreement.

Making this distinction steers you clear of a big trap—plunging in to resolve *the wrong problem.*

A *misunderstanding* is a failure to understand each other accurately. A *true disagreement* is a failure to agree that would persist despite the most accurate understanding.

In a misunderstanding, the solution is simple: you understand each other accurately, the problem disappears. In a true disagreement, you need a strategy to persuade them.

Try to solve the wrong problem, and you risk making things worse. For example, suppose you've got a true disagreement. Suppose the other person already knows your point of view. If you treat the issue as a misunderstanding, and you keep explaining your view over and over because you think they don't understand, they may just get annoyed at you and dig in— the Talking Trap.

Now suppose the problem is still a true disagreement. The other person wants you to change. But suppose that in this new scenario, you invite them to explain their concerns, while you listen carefully, understand them, and then do nothing. What are they likely to do? Get even *more* upset with you!

It was bad enough that you weren't willing to change when you were ignorant. But now that you've been enlightened by their point of view and you still aren't willing to change...well, that's downright galling. Thus, in a true disagreement, if you listen, understand them, and then stand firm, you won't settle anything—and you can easily make things worse.

I'd like you to picture a typical quiet suburban neighborhood. It's Brady-Bunch perfect. One morning, neighbors wake up to hear: jackhammers and a bulldozer in a vacant lot. A sign says: "Site of New County Probation Facility."

Probation facility!!?

The neighbors call the county. They don't want

criminals in their backyard! They want this project *stopped.*

The county's chief deputy probation officer figures: "Legally, I can keep building, but for the sake of community relations, I'll hold a meeting to clear up their misconceptions, then they'll all go home and the problem will go away." Classic example of the Great Myth of Hidden Harmony. And you can probably guess what happened.

The chief deputy, Mr. Feemley, held his meeting at 7 p.m. at the high-school auditorium. Reporters for all three TV stations were there, along with 100 angry neighbors. Mr. Feemley faced them and said, "You people don't understand! No hard criminals will be coming here. Serious offenders aren't even eligible for probation!"

A woman called out, "What's serious?"

Mr. Feemley reassured her, "No rapists or murderers. Just the minor offenders. I have a list of them." He began handing out copies.

It took only a minute for someone to pipe up, "Hey, this list includes *drug dealers, child molesters, and burglars!*"

Mr. Feemley explained, "Yes, but these people are trying to go straight. These are the *good* criminals!"

As the laughing and booing died down, Mr. Feemley realized: this was not simply a misunderstanding.

True, the neighbors had a misconception: they thought that "hardened criminals" were the same as "probationers." To Mr. Feemley, there was a big difference between the two groups: probationers were convicted of lesser offenses, and probationers were trying to go straight.

He was sure that the neighbors' opposition was based on their confusion of the two groups. If only he explained the distinction, he would eliminate the confusion, and thus eliminate the opposition.

So he did explain, the neighbors did understand, the confusion was eliminated, but the problem remained.

Why?

Because to the neighbors, the distinction between "hardened criminals" and "probationers" was a distinction without a difference. They were *all* criminals. And the people in that auditorium did not want *any* criminals in their neighborhood. So all of Mr. Feemley's explanations could not solve the problem. He and the neighbors had a conflict in goals. That conflict—not a misunderstanding—was the root of the problem.

He wanted the probationers there.

The neighbors did not.

This difference would not go away with more explaining and listening. On the contrary. The more he talked, and the more the neighbors talked, the *angrier* they became.

One angry neighbor after another was parading up to the podium, and Mr. Feemley was telling each speaker, "We hear you, we hear you." Finally, someone stood up and shouted: "You say you've heard us? *Stop construction!*"

Mr. Feemley was speechless, unprepared to handle this true disagreement.

"I can't stop construction," he finally admitted.

"What?!" the neighbor shouted, "You liar! You said you'd *listen* to us! Why did you even hold this meeting??"

"Well," Mr. Feemley said, looking at the floor, "We wanted to give you a chance to vent."

I thought the crowd was going to lynch the man.

This chief deputy had to defend himself to three TV reporters, the city council, and his own county board of supervisors, all because he treated a true disagreement as a misunderstanding.

The Myth of the Miracle Meeting

Mr. Feemley is not alone. Many managers are seduced by the Myth of the Miracle Meeting, in which controversies large and small are supposed to vanish, thanks to the magic of understanding.

Let me assure you, when it comes to true disagreements, real life does not work this way.

I'm reminded of this fact whenever I give presentations at conferences. People in the audience ask me, "David, whenever there's a problem at work, my boss always makes everyone get together for a meeting to understand each other. But at the end of the meeting, things are often *worse*. Why is that?"

Because: In a true disagreement, listening and explaining are not enough to resolve the problem.

In a true disagreement, if you hold a meeting to

improve understanding, you accomplish only one of two things: (a) you do no good whatsoever, or (b) you make things worse.

Frequently, you make things worse.

Why is this so? Because when you listen and explain, it's easy to fall into the Talking Trap. In the process of improving understanding, *your meeting can actually provide a forum for people to fight each other.* That's exactly what happened in the case of the probation facility. By holding a meeting, Mr. Feemley provided a forum for people to fight him. He fell into the Talking Trap. In a true disagreement, improving understanding can produce deadlock.

Let me underscore this: It is absolutely, positively, not possible—repeat, not possible—to resolve a true disagreement by understanding each other better.

In a true disagreement, people want more than your explanations. More than your listening. More than your understanding.

They want you to *change your mind.*

So before you rush to clarify communication, stop to consider what type of problem you're facing.

How to identify the problem

Often a misunderstanding overlies a true disagreement and masks it, so it's not obvious. The neighbors said, "We want you to *listen and understand us.*" So that was what Mr. Feemley thought he literally needed to do.

He held the meeting to listen to them, so they would have the satisfaction of being heard—and also to clear up their confusion between "hardened criminals" and "probationers." He was sure that listening and explaining would solve the problem. He did not recognize the underlying true disagreement about whether *any* criminals should be in that neighborhood at all.

Many problems resemble an iceberg: on the surface, you see poor understanding; just underneath, out of sight, lurks a true disagreement.

So how can you distinguish a true disagreement from a misunderstanding?

A simple test. Ask yourself: *"Would the problem disappear if we understood each other better?"*

In other words...

- If you succeeded in explaining yourself, would the other person change their mind?
- If you only listened and understood them, would they feel satisfied and stop opposing you?
- If they explained themselves more to you, would you change your position?

If your answer to any of these questions is yes, then you have a misunderstanding, and greater understanding could help.

If your answer is no, you've got a true disagreement. As in Mr. Feemley's predicament, you may also have a misunderstanding, but the key is that *in a true disagreement, better understanding won't resolve the whole problem.* Listening and explaining could clear up the superficial misunderstanding—about who was eligible for probation; but the underlying true disagreement remained—about whether the facility should be built.

Examples applying the test

Here's a marriage that was in trouble immediately. Jill had just married Hank, a psychologist. Right after their wedding, they drove off to a resort cottage to begin their honeymoon.

The next morning, Jill sneaked off to the kitchen to make breakfast. She had an image of the two of them spooning food into each other's mouths, kissing and discussing how much they were looking forward to spending the rest of their lives together.

This is not what happened. When she brought his breakfast on a tray to the bedroom, she saw her loved one in bed *reading the newspaper.* She set the meal on the covers in front of him.

He did not put down the newspaper.

She slipped off her robe and climbed naked into bed next to him and began caressing his shoulder.

He did not put down the newspaper.

She *asked* him to put down the newspaper. Several times. Each time he said, "Uh, just a minute hon—" and kept reading.

It did not matter to her why he was continuing to read. This man, to whom she had just committed to spending the rest of her life, wanted the *newspaper* more than her! And on their honeymoon!!!

To his credit, Hank the psychologist did notice that his wife was now displaying the warmth and vivacity of dry ice. His eyes stayed glued to the sports section, but from his mouth came the innocent words: "Honey...is anything *wrong?*"

She grabbed the newspaper out of his hands and yelled: "Yes! There is something *WRONG!* On the morning after our wedding I want to cuddle and talk and all you can think about is the *newspaper???!!*"

Hank the psychologist smiled knowingly, "That's how I thought you were feeling. Let me reassure you, I share your intention to affirm our closeness. However, to do that, I do not feel the need for us to talk and touch each other. Having you by my side is all I need."

"Well, *I* need more. I don't care about your intentions; I care what you *do.*"

"Well, what I'd like to do is read the newspaper."

"I think you've made that abundantly clear." She rose from the bed. "I'm going for a walk."

She slammed the door.

Now, could this problem have disappeared if Jill had understood Hank better?

You might think so. If only she had understood how important it was to him to read the newspaper, if only she had understood that he truly cared about her, she might not have exploded.

But this theory overlooks Jill's own words: "I don't care about your intentions; I care what you *do.*"

This was a true disagreement about how to spend the first hours of their honeymoon: she wanted to cuddle; he preferred to read the paper. The problem subsided only when Hank agreed not to look at another newspaper for the rest of their trip.

He had to change his behavior to resolve things. Greater understanding was not enough.

NOW LOOK AT THIS NEXT CASE. Bob has gotten a new job and has to move. Unfortunately, he's just signed a one-year lease. He reads it and discovers—surprise!—there's no penalty for leaving early. So Bob gives his notice, packs up and leaves.

A few weeks later, at his new home, Bob gets a bill from his old landlord for an extra month's rent. A note explains it's a fee for breaking his contract.

Bob calls up the landlord. "I can't see anywhere that I've got to pay one month's rent as a breaking-contract charge."

The landlord explains, "Actually, you owe for the whole year. That's what a one-year contract means."

Bob responds, *"One-year* means that the whole contract is good for one year. The contract includes the termination clause on page two. That says only that I've got to give you one month's notice, which I did." Bob reads the clause to her. "You understand?"

"Sure I understand!" The landlord repeats, "You owe for the whole year! I'm being nice, charging you for only one extra month. I could be charging you for ten extra months. If you're refusing to pay, I'll turn the whole thing over to my attorneys. Perhaps you'd like to speak to them."

"I'm not refusing to pay," Bob replies calmly, "if you can show me where it says I'm supposed to."

Now, the test: Would this problem disappear if these two people could understand each other better?

You'd be tempted to say yes. After all, this is a matter of presenting information in black-and-white, right?

Wrong. Bob has done that. It hasn't gotten him anywhere. Landlord and tenant understand each other. They both think that they are right. This is true-disagreement territory.

There's an assumption that you will win an argument if you prove you are right.

Not so in a true disagreement.

Being right is not enough. In a true disagreement, it doesn't matter whether the facts are on your side. The other person will not budge.

People think an argument is a battle to discover who is correct. Often, it's a battle to discover who is more stubborn. Truth is just another weapon in the battle. It is no magic wand. It cannot make a true disagreement—poof!—disappear.

Case in point: I bought a station wagon whose rear door kept falling off every six months. It would get unhinged, I'd take it to the dealer, we'd agree there was a design defect, and he'd repair the door under the warranty.

The fourth time my door fell off, the dealer happened to mention: his repair jobs had been *temporary.* Of course, I knew that was how they had turned out, but I never thought it had been on purpose.

I asked, how about fixing the door permanently this time? He said no, a permanent repair was not factory-authorized under the warranty, because the manufacturer would not admit there was a defect.

Again, the test: Would the problem with the dealer have disappeared if we'd understood each other better?

Not a chance. We did understand each other: I wanted him to repair my door permanently under the warranty; he refused because he wouldn't get reimbursed by the manufacturer.

We had a true disagreement.

The dealer even admitted, "David, you're right. If your door keeps falling off, it *should* be repaired free."

But to him, whether I was right did not matter. What mattered was his pocketbook. He understood the rightness of my position. That understanding was not enough to resolve the issue.

Can you settle a true disagreement with facts?

Conventional wisdom says yes:	Strategic communication says no:
An argument is a battle to discover who is factually correct.	Often, an argument is a battle to discover who is more stubborn.
Truth will make any disagreement disappear.	Truth is just another weapon in the battle.
All that matters is whether you are right.	Whether you are right may not matter at all.
If the facts are on your side, you will prevail.	Facts are not enough when your goals collide.

CROSS-FADE TO COLEMAN, TEXAS. It's a Sunday afternoon in July and 104 degrees. There's a dust storm outside. Fortunately, Jerry and his wife are inside, playing dominoes at her parents' house.

Suddenly her father suggests, "Let's drive to Abilene and get dinner at the cafeteria."

Jerry thinks, "What?? Drive 53 miles? In this dust and heat? In an unairconditioned 1958 Buick with vinyl seats?"

But he does not say this. Instead, Jerry turns to his wife and asks politely, "Dear, what would *you* like to do?"

Jerry's wife smiles, "Sounds great to me! Mom?"

Mom chimes in, "Of course I want to go! I haven't been to Abilene in a long time!"

So: These four human beings, specimens of this planet's most intelligent life form, all voluntarily squeeze into an unairconditioned car to go 106 miles across a godforsaken desert with the temperature of a furnace.

When they trudge back into the living room four hours later, they are all covered with a layer of dust that is cemented by perspiration.

"I guess we all arrived 'home cooked.' Ha-hah!" This is Jerry's idea of a joke, to lighten the mood.

Silence.

At last, Mom pipes up, irritated: "I wish we'd stayed here. I went along only because you all pressured me into it."

Jerry's wife looks shocked. "What do you mean 'you all'? I went only because Jerry and Dad wanted to go."

Jerry blurts out, "Hey, don't blame me! I went to satisfy you!"

Now Dad enters the fray. "Hell! I never wanted to

go. I thought you might be bored here. I was enjoying dominoes."

Would this problem have disappeared if people had understood each other better?

Absolutely. There was no disagreement. They all agreed when the trip was proposed: they did *not* want to go. But they all kept their preferences to themselves, out of politeness.

Result: They all thought everyone else wanted to go, so they said they wanted to go, too. They all said they wanted to go, when in fact, *nobody* wanted to go.

This was a colossal misunderstanding.

Look behind the words. But even when people are saying what they're thinking, even when their words seem perfectly clear, even when there appears on the surface to be no likelihood whatsoever that the problem is a misunderstanding...it may still be a misunderstanding.

How is that possible?

Let's look at one example. In San Francisco during the Vietnam War, an African-American leader made a speech against President Nixon's Vietnam policy. He shouted, "We will kill Richard Nixon."

Sounds clear, doesn't it? He was threatening to kill the president. That's what he was arrested and indicted for. But the defense claimed he was innocent; it was all a misunderstanding.

Was the defense right? Would this problem have disappeared if the police had understood him better?

The case was dismissed on a technicality; but according to a noted anthropologist from the University of California, Berkeley, the answer was: yes, this was a misunderstanding.

He said blacks in the area were interviewed about how they used the verb *kill.* Their answers were almost all metaphors, such as "He's killing me" (with laughter), "Kill it" (meaning 'stop doing that'), or "That killed him around here" (meaning 'that destroyed his influence'). Nobody answered that *kill* had anything to do with taking someone's life.

Then the blacks were asked: How *would* they say that they wanted to murder someone? Again, they responded with metaphors like "wipe him out," "rip him off," and "waste him."

So when the speaker said "kill Richard Nixon," he meant "destroy his influence." He'd been using a local dialect, different from standard English. Later, watching a videotape of his address, the speaker admitted, "I blew it."

You might say this is an unusually tricky example of distinguishing a misunderstanding from a true disagreement. But in such a tricky case, how can you avoid the mistake the police made of misjudging the situation?

First, *recognize that a literal interpretation is not always the accurate one.* Consider: Does a literal interpretation leave some questions unanswered? Here, one unanswered question is: Why would someone intending to murder the president announce it on a public platform? That should give you a clue that to understand this speaker, you may have to look beyond his literal words.

Then, *interpret what the other person says in the context of their communication style*, their normal way of expressing themselves. Could the other person have been trying to send a different message than the one you received? If you're dealing across cultures, you may need to consult someone who knows the other culture.

When people don't want to understand. When communication is cloudy, sometimes people prefer to remain in the fog. They don't ask, "What do you mean?" because if they understood the true message, they're afraid they wouldn't like it. So they remain ignorant and avoid facing reality.

Take the case of my client Lisa, an executive who had to hire an administrative assistant. She waded through resumes, interviewed seven people, and found only one good applicant—a guy named Jeff.

She called him back for a second interview. She began with some chitchat: "I see from your resume you moved here recently."

Jeff said, "Yeah, two months ago."

"And how do you like it?"

"Well, I love the city, but my wife's schedule makes life crazy. She's a nurse and works evenings—which means I've got to pick up our three kids from day care every night at five o'clock and feed them dinner."

Lisa nodded sympathetically. "My husband and I were on different schedules for several months. Now we both work until eight at night."

Then they went on to discuss the position, Jeff seemed to be the perfect candidate, and Lisa gave him the job.

Within six weeks she regretted that decision.

She ordered Jeff into her office and closed the door. "We need to discuss your lack of commitment to your job."

Jeff was astounded. "Lack of commitment??"

Lisa continued, "You leave every day at 5 p.m., no matter how much work there is."

Jeff protested, "But I told you I have to pick up my kids from day care and give them dinner. When you hired me, you understood I'd have to leave at 5 p.m."

Lisa replied, "And I told *you* that I work until eight. You're my administrative assistant and I need you here. After all, this is a *job*. Work comes before family!"

Jeff didn't know what to do.

For that matter, neither did Lisa. She called me and asked: Should she clarify communication with Jeff about the requirements of his job? I said, "That depends whether you have a misunderstanding or a true disagreement. What *was* your understanding about job hours?"

She sighed, "Honestly, it wasn't clear. You see, I really wanted to hire him. I was reluctant to make an issue about hours because I might scare him off. And he didn't raise the issue because he needed the job."

In other words, both people chose to skirt the subject and interpret the situation the way they wanted. Jeff chose to assume he could leave at five, and Lisa chose to assume he had tacitly agreed to work until eight.

So: Would this problem disappear if only they understood each other better?

No.

True, they misunderstood each other—deliberately. But now, even if they each explained what they meant, they would not agree, because they never had. On the subject of work hours, they had a true disagreement, going all the way back to the job interview.

Some disagreements are hidden intentionally

I was visiting a company on a consulting assignment when the sales manager pulled me aside and asked, "I'm having problems with Dingler in manufacturing. We can't seem to understand each other. I think he should take a course in effective listening. What do you think?"

I asked her, "What's the problem?"

She said, "Dingler doesn't listen to me."

I asked, "Do you know *why* he doesn't listen?"

She reflected for a moment. "He says it's because I constantly insult him."

I asked, "Do you mean to insult him?"

She nodded, "Sometimes, sure. Like yesterday, when Dingler refused to change the manufacturing schedule to meet a deadline for our largest customer. Our *largest* customer! I couldn't believe it. The man is so dumb, if he had a brain, he'd play with it. I told him so."

"I see. Tell me, what reason did Dingler give for refusing to change the schedule?"

"He complained about paying the overtime."

I concluded, "He doesn't need a course in effective listening. It won't address the root problem. When you insult him again, he's *still* going to tune you out.

"The problem is not poor listening skills. He is capable of listening when he wants to. He knows how. He is *choosing* not to listen to you because you're insulting him. And you're insulting him because of his position on overtime."

"You are understanding each other, all right. It's because you understand his position that you insult him. And it's because he understands your insults that he ignores you."

"To get him to listen to you, you need to address the *reason* he is not listening. You need to stop insulting him and work out your true disagreement about overtime. When you resolve that issue, the communication difficulty will disappear: you won't feel the need to insult him, and he won't ignore you."

The sales manager thought about that. "I see your point. But I don't want to confront the subject of overtime because Dingler will demand I pay for it!"

This manager preferred to call the problem a "listening issue" so she could avoid dealing with the true disagreement and thus avoid paying the overtime cost.

Her strategy is the same one used by Senior Management at the rocket manufacturer where the employee, Tom Shackleberry, complained about executive salaries. Virgil W. Grimm, VP for Human Resources, avoided dealing with that true disagreement the same way—by treating it as a communication issue. Grimm said that Shackleberry needed a "full explanation."

Five reasons people camouflage disagreement

There are at least five major reasons people like to make believe they have "misunderstandings" or "communication issues" instead of "disagreements."

1. If they don't admit there's a conflict, maybe they can avoid facing it. This was the premise of Grimm's strategy. If he didn't admit that Shackleberry had a conflict with management, maybe the company could avoid dealing with it.

2. People think they project a more positive image if they come across as not having any disagreements. If others know that you're in a disagreement, they may think you are personally disagreeable. They may blame you for the problem. To preserve your reputation, you may choose to conceal the fact that you and your spouse have a true disagreement. A true disagreement in the marriage? That's like saying the marriage is in trouble. That could reflect badly on both of you.

Instead, you say, "We're having a little misunderstanding." We're not resolving a dispute, we're having a discussion. We're not negotiating, we're working things out.

3. It can appear rude to acknowledge a disagreement explicitly. The other person may take offense if you openly dispute their point of view. If you set up a confrontation and win, they may lose face.

Thus, it can seem much more polite to deny that the two of you have any real difference of opinion and to dismiss any apparent difference as a misunderstanding.

4. People hide their disagreement to defuse your anger. Jimmy wanted to go out with his friends to play. His mom told him to be home by six for dinner. Jimmy privately disagreed about when to return; he wanted to stay out until sunset. But he did not say anything. Instead, he simply stayed out late—and then played innocent: "Honest, Mom! I didn't disobey you on purpose! I misunderstood! I thought you said *seven* o'clock, not six!" He figured, "How can Mom get mad at me for an honest misunderstanding?"

5. People pretend you have a "misunderstanding" to make you share the blame for it. When Jimmy demurred, "I thought you said *seven* o'clock, not six!" he was not only trying to defuse Mom's anger. He was also trying to make her share the blame for his tardiness: "Gee...I guess we had a misunderstanding. I suppose we'll *both* have to be clearer next time."

As if her communication had been part of the problem.

How to uncover a true disagreement

If you're dealing with someone who wants to pretend there is no conflict, they will not tell you if they have a dispute with you. You can ask them, "Do we have a misunderstanding or do we disagree?" but you won't get an honest answer. To help you identify the type of problem, here are some questions to consider:

Do your goals conflict? Does the other person have a reason for acting against your wishes? Jimmy certainly had a motive for staying out late: he got to play longer with his friends.

Does the other person benefit by downplaying the problem? Based on the five reasons people camouflage disagreement, ask yourself:

- Would this person want to avoid dealing with a true disagreement?
- Would they like to project a more positive image by pretending there is no conflict?
- Would they prefer to smooth things over for the sake of politeness?
- Would they conceal their disagreement to assuage your anger?
- Would they call it a "misunderstanding" to imply you are partly to blame?

Does this person have a history of hiding disagreement? This was the tip-off to Jimmy's mom. She saw that his behavior was part of a pattern. He regularly claimed to "misunderstand" her whenever he disagreed with her—regardless of whether the issue was being home on time, emptying the dishwasher, or taking out the garbage. That was enough to set off alarm bells that his tardiness was more than a misunderstanding.

If you're dealing with someone for the first time and you're not sure how to read their behavior, consult *How do you uncover someone's perceptions?*, page 128.

Is poor communication the problem?

Conventional wisdom:	Strategic communication:
There is no conflict, only poor communication.	In a true disagreement, there is often plenty of communication.
People who disagree do not understand each other.	People who disagree often *do* understand each other—and that's why they stop talking.
Poor communication is the cause of all interpersonal problems.	Poor communication is often the *result* of the problem, not the cause.

WHEN YOU IDENTIFY A PROBLEM as a true disagreement, you avoid futilely trying to resolve it by improving understanding. By identifying the type of problem, you determine the right approach for resolving it. (In a misunderstanding, you need to improve understanding; in a true disagreement, you must develop a strategy to persuade them.)

Next, to work toward a solution, you've got to establish a goal. But not for yourself.

For the *other* person.

❖ *Key points for applying strategic step #1:*
Decide whether you have a misunderstanding or a true disagreement

1. Remember that *more understanding will help only if lack of understanding is the problem.* Often, as in the

Talking Trap, poor communication is the *result*—not the *cause.*

2. Ask yourself: *"Would the problem disappear if we understood each other better?"* If so, you have a misunderstanding; if not, there is a true disagreement.

3. If the other person is hiding a true disagreement, use these questions to help you uncover it:
   - Do your goals conflict?
   - Does the other person benefit by downplaying the problem? (Review the *five reasons people camouflage disagreement.*)
   - Does this person have a history of hiding disagreement?

4. Beware of taking the "We Can Work It Out" approach—believing that if only the other person understands you, they'll agree with you. It may work in some misunderstandings, but never in a true disagreement.

5. Avoid trying to change the other person's mind. That's one of the hardest ways to resolve an argument. Remember: *People prefer to reinterpret the facts to suit their preconceptions rather than to admit they're wrong.*

Create the other person's next move

Developing a strategy requires setting a goal. But when it comes to working with people, the way we've been taught to set goals is backwards. We've been taught to decide what WE will do. We should first focus on what we want THEM to do.

Ｈow do you get a pay raise?

Conventional wisdom says you communicate. You gather facts about how good a job you're doing and show the boss you deserve more. My student Marilyn tried doing that. Officially, her job title was "secretary," but she prepared a presentation showing her department head that she was really doing the work of an administrator and that with all her accomplishments she deserved a 7% raise.

Her department head, Mike, listened to her and smiled gently: "Marilyn, you do excellent work. You know I'd like to help. I'd *like* to give you a 7% raise. Unfortunately," he sighed and spread open his arms, "there's no budget for me to give you a raise."

"But...but..." Marilyn tried several counter-arguments.

Nothing worked.

Marilyn walked out of his office in a daze. She could not fathom how, with such a convincing presentation, with Mike *agreeing* with her that she deserved a 7% raise, she had nonetheless somehow been defeated by three words, "there's no budget"! How did that happen? Where did she go wrong?

It's not enough to know what you want

Certainly, Marilyn erred by treating the issue as a misunderstanding. She assumed that after she presented the facts, Mike would give her a 7% raise. But she

made another common mistake: while Marilyn knew
that she wanted more money, she neglected to consider what Mike should *do* to help her get it.

What was he supposed to do—call up the division
manager and say, "Remember the money for raises I
spent last spring? Well, I sorta made a mistake. Can I
have more money for Marilyn?" Mike wouldn't want
to appear so irresponsible.

What, specifically, was he supposed to do for her?

She assumed this was a trivial detail. She assumed
that if he wanted to give her more pay, he would *know*
what to do.

As Marilyn discovered, if the other person doesn't
know what to do, they may fail to do it.

So *you* need to do the work of figuring out specifically what you want the other person to do. *The less
work for them to do, the more likely they are to do it.* (Of
course, you don't want to alienate the other person by
giving orders. Make your request sensitively. But unless you know what you want them to do, you cannot
intentionally approach them to do it.)

I said to Marilyn, "Let's think about what Mike
could do to get you more pay. Why don't you find
out all the ways that exist in this company for a manager to give an employee more money."

Next week she came back and reported: "I talked to
a friend of mine in Human Resources. She says the final decision is not up to Mike. The division manager
has to approve it. However, Mike could request that I
get a *reclassification.* You see, I'm working beyond my

job description as a secretary; I'm really doing the work of an administrator. If my job were reclassified as administrative, I'd get more pay."

Bingo. Marilyn should have asked for a reclassification, not a raise. You might think Marilyn's problem was she didn't know what she wanted. But she did know. She knew she wanted more pay.

Her problem was she didn't know *what she wanted the other person to do for her.*

Once she knew she wanted Mike to request a reclassification, he did so, the division manager approved it, and she got her increase—in fact, double the raise she had sought. As an administrator, she earned 14% more.

The moral?

It's strategic step #2: *Create the other person's next move.*

What—*specifically*—should they do?

Sometimes you believe you have identified what you want the other person to do for you—but in reality, you haven't. Because the action that you want them to take is far too vague.

I'll give you an example. Julia and Herb co-founded a small company together, but recently, they've begun feuding and now they're even threatening to sue each other. Julia says she won't sue, if Herb makes a "reasonable attempt to reach agreement soon."

Just a moment. "A reasonable attempt to reach agreement soon"? What does that mean?

If Herb agrees to meet but doesn't concede anything, is that "reasonable"? And what is "soon"? If Herb is busy this week but is willing to meet next week, would Julia think that was "soon" enough?

Julia admitted to me she wasn't sure. Her words were vague because her thinking was vague. Until she could distill in her own mind what she wanted Herb to do, there was little hope she could get him to do it.

No wonder that whenever they got together for a meeting, nothing good would come of it.

We've all been to meetings where everyone shows up with no clear idea of what they want anyone to do. They want the other person to "do something constructive" or "make an offer."

"Make an offer"? If the person makes *any* offer, will you be satisfied? What terms would you like to see?

Get specific. *Before the meeting, consider: What precisely would the person have to do, for you to perceive there was progress?* Once you crystallize your objective, you can think strategically about how to approach them.

But if everyone walks into the conference room without a clear goal, what typically happens?

A lot of frustration, that's what.

Someone turns to you and exclaims, "Just *tell* me! *What* do you want me to do??!" Since you don't know, you find yourself asking, "Well, uh, what do *you* suggest?" The question of what to do becomes a hot potato that you toss back and forth across the table, because *nobody* has a clue about what to do.

No wonder talking doesn't get us anywhere. No

wonder meetings are reputed to be colossal wastes of time.

The Selfishness Syndrome

The benefit of creating the other person's next move is clear. Yet often we instinctively avoid doing it.

Why?

One client of mine, an attorney, explained, *"I'm* going to do what *my* side wants. I'm not going to worry about the other guys!"

It's a law of human nature: when we get under stress and emotionally consumed by a problem, we become self-centered. When we're upset at the other person, we don't feel like paying attention to them at all. We don't care about designing a move for them to make. That's the furthest thing from our mind.

We focus entirely on ourselves and on what *we* are going to do.

This is precisely the error that my friend Jack made when his wife left him.

She called him a few days after leaving, suggesting that they get together at a cafe to talk things over. Jack thought a lot about that meeting beforehand. He said, "I knew I wanted to be cold and aloof to show her I didn't need her." Result: she saw him as cold and aloof, concluded he didn't need her, and eventually divorced him.

She did the opposite of what he wanted, because he was so busy posturing to satisfy his pride that he failed to consider what he wanted his wife to do.

The battle cry is "I'll show them!" But "showing them" makes no sense at all unless they *do* something for you as a result.

When you're trying to influence someone, your goal is not to indulge your emotions.

It's to get results.

Adopting any posture, aloof or warm, is useful only if it helps you achieve your goal. Don't lose sight of your goal. Your goal is for *them* to do something.

When you're stuck in an interpersonal problem, the first question you may be tempted to ask yourself is, "What should *I* do?" But to influence someone, you need to ask a different question: "What do I want the *other* person to do?"

So don't immediately try to determine the proper stance to take or the right attitude to adopt when the other person walks in the room. First things first. You need to figure out what you want the other person to do for you.

Remember: The next move *you* should make depends on the next move you want *them* to make.

Select the right person

Note that I've been referring to "the other person," not "the corporation" or "the other side." That's no accident. Because while strategic communication has been applied successfully to problems involving large institutions, you can run into a lot of trouble trying to influence everyone in the same room at the same time—even if they are all from the same organization!

In complex cases, some of the people across the table from you may be fighting each other, and when you say something to appeal to one person, you may alienate someone else.

When you're afraid this might happen, it's best to focus on one key person at a time and develop a strategy tailored to each individual. You may still decide to approach each key person around the same time; but by approaching them one-on-one, you avoid the difficult dynamics of a large group.

Now, in your particular situation, you may think there is no question about whom to deal with. That's what Marilyn thought. She figured that her boss was the only one she had to approach.

But she was mistaken. Before talking to him, Marilyn first had to consult a friend of hers in Human Resources to discover the company's mechanisms for increasing pay.

Even if your issue seems to involve only you and the person you want to influence, you may need to talk to someone else—perhaps to gain support, or perhaps, as in Marilyn's case, to gain information. Consequently, the best person to approach isn't always the obvious one.

For example, let's say you need to return a suit you bought yesterday, only a sign in the store says: "NO REFUNDS, NO EXCHANGES, NEVER." You eye the cashier behind the counter. She's the obvious person to approach, right? When I give this problem to my students, they try to influence the cashier.

They get nowhere.

The cashier can't make an exception to store policy. She'd be fired. She has the power only to point to the sign that says, "NO, NO, NEVER." That's the only power she has. Her mission is to discourage you.

Don't get stuck with someone who can only say no. Find out who has the power to say yes.

Two rules for making your selection. The person you approach must be *influential* enough to help you get what you want, and *receptive* enough to listen to you. *Influential* and *receptive.* Those are your two criteria for picking the right person.

To find someone influential and receptive, consider:

- *Who is the ultimate decision-maker?* (In Marilyn's case, it was the division manager.)
- *Whom does that person depend upon for advice or support?* (The division manager relied on Marilyn's boss Mike for recommendations. Mike relied on Human Resources to learn about the company's system for giving increases.)
- *Who would see things your way?* (Mike was sympathetic; so was Marilyn's buddy in HR.)
- *With whom do you have a good working relationship?*

Now let's apply these two criteria—influential and receptive—to select the right person for you to approach in another situation:

Your neighbor Henry has been living next door for six years. You see him every few months at a neighborhood potluck dinner with his sister Henrietta, who visits him all the time. During these social occasions you've observed that the two of them are close and he seems to respect her opinion a lot. You've also discovered that Henry is an ardent environmentalist. He's a member of a group called Friends of the City Forest that goes around planting trees to beautify the city. His sister considers him idealistic; she smiles at his endeavors but never joins in.

Recently you've become concerned about the magnificent oak tree in Henry's back yard. The tree spreads its bountiful branches not only over his roof but also over yours, and with your luck, those big branches will come crashing down during the next storm and damage your house. Henry's tree will have to go. You see him gardening one Sunday and you think, "Why not go up to him now and talk about his tree?"

Why not? He's the *wrong person,* that's why not.

Sure, it's his tree, and he's the obvious person to approach. But not the *best* person. You know that Henry is a staunch protector of trees. He'd hate the idea of *pruning* the tree. He would consider it dismemberment of a living creature. He meets the criterion of being *influential;* he is, after all, the final decision-maker here. But he would not be *receptive* to you.

His sister, on the other hand, is likely to be both *influential* with Henry and more *receptive* to your concerns. In fact, she may share your concerns. She may be worried about the branches hanging over Henry's roof. And you've observed that she has a lot of influence with him. So you decide to approach her at the next potluck dinner.

A cautionary note about selecting whom to approach: Sometimes there is an official representative you are supposed to deal with. And if you go over that person's head, you can make a powerful enemy.

But what if this official representative refuses to help you? Don't give up yet. Perhaps a friend of yours can contact someone else in the organization, so *you* don't make enemies. Or, perhaps you can find someone to influence the official representative for you.

The point is, if you're not making progress with the person you're talking to, do what Marilyn did: Consider, for the time being, focusing on somebody else.

Get realistic about what they are willing and able to do

When Syl was seven years old, she liked to play schoolteacher. She brought out the blackboard and wrote the word *cat* on it. She tried to get her three-year-old sister, Alice, to write the word *cat*. Alice started to cry.

Syl screamed, "You're not trying hard enough!"

Their mother took Syl aside and told her, "Alice can't write the word *cat*. Her brain hasn't developed far enough for her to write letters. It has nothing to do with trying. The brain has to grow the way the body does. Do you think that when Alice was six months old, she could've walked if only she had tried?"

Sylvia replied, "Of course not, she wasn't ready."

Mom said, "Exactly. And right now, her brain isn't ready for writing. But because you can't see her brain, you can't tell that it isn't ready."

Our attempts to influence people often fail because we're asking them to do something they're not ready or able to do. Sometimes the impediment is physical, sometimes it's mental. Sometimes it's a lack of ability, sometimes it's a lack of willingness. But this lack of ability or readiness isn't always obvious. So, like Syl, we may fail to recognize it.

Recognizing the other person's limit is vital to developing a realistic move they can make. But there's a problem with the way we've been taught to assess someone's limit. There's a difference between what the other person can do right now and what they might ultimately do.

Focus on their *immediate limit*, not their "bottom line." Suppose you are renting your house to Rhoda for $750 a month. She's paid $750 a month for the last five years. Now you want to boost it to $1000, and she's balking. You know that you've got to create a realistic move for Rhoda to make, but how can you gauge what's realistic?

Here's the textbook answer: You need to discover Rhoda's "bottom line"—the most she would pay for renting your house. Her bottom line is the most she'd ultimately be willing and able to do to satisfy you. Suppose you figure out that Rhoda could pay $950 a month. This means that agreeing to pay $950 is a realistic move for her to make...right?

Not necessarily.

Remember, Rhoda's bottom line is the most she could do for you *ultimately*. Ultimately, she might accept $950. But she may not be willing to agree to that *immediately*. She's used to paying $750 and believes that's fair. For Rhoda, accepting a $200 increase today is too big a step too soon.

You've got to consider Rhoda's *immediate limit*— the most she is willing and able to do for you *right now*. Perhaps the most that Rhoda is willing to do right now is to review some classified ads with you, so together you can determine the market rate for renting comparable homes.

If she becomes convinced she can't find a similar house for less than $950, and if she recognizes that a rent increase is overdue, *then* she may be ready to consider paying $950. But before she's willing to consider that, she has to take several smaller mental steps first.

The danger of focusing on their bottom line. You can't expect someone to make a move that might be possible eventually but which is *im*possible now. Let's say that Rhoda isn't ready to consider any increase right now. Her immediate limit is to review classified ads with you.

If you keep pushing for her to accept $950 a month right now, she might call the movers.

That's the danger of focusing on the other person's bottom line: if you ask for too much now, the other person may balk and refuse to budge at all.

A common mistake is automatically to press for everything you want all at once. I was speaking to foreign executives at the University of California, Berkeley, when one manager suggested, "If you want Rhoda to agree to $950 a month, you should go in asking for $1200!" He said that you should ask for more than you want, so that you have room to compromise.

This strategy overlooks Rhoda's immediate limit. She is not ready to consider *any* increase right now. Her immediate limit is to review the classifieds with you. That's the most you can get her to do right now.

If you ignore that reality and push for her bottom line, you will accomplish nothing, except perhaps to alienate her.

Set your goal at her immediate limit, not her bottom line. You should be trying to get her to do the most she is willing and able to do for you *right now*.

You can do the impossible...right?

Conventional wisdom:	Strategic communication:
Anything is possible if you *believe* it is possible.	If you push for the impossible, it will still be impossible.
Where there is a will, there is a way.	When you ignore their will, they may fight you all the way.
Shoot for the stars.	Recognize reality.

How to uncover someone's immediate limit

One way to determine someone's immediate limit is simply to reflect, "What's the most I can get them to do right now?" But if you're having trouble answering that question, there are three techniques you can use.

Examining their perceptions. The most that someone is willing to do for you depends on their views, attitudes, and beliefs about the situation. How much do *they* believe they should do for you at this point in time? (The next chapter provides seven techniques for uncovering someone's perceptions.)

Testing by pushing. This is the most direct method to gauge how big a move you can get someone to make. You make a proposal or take a stand and see whether they budge. If they absolutely refuse, you know you've reached their immediate limit.

Testing by pushing can be a very useful tool when, for example, you are trying to get your husband to clean up the garage. You broach the subject over breakfast, as he is champing down his Wheaties. You begin by stating a fact: "The garage needs to be cleaned up."

In between mouthfuls he acknowledges: "Yeah, it does."

Aha! You've gotten him to *admit* that the garage needs to be cleaned up! This itself is an accomplishment.

Then you suggest, "How about going out there and getting rid of all those old magazines you're never going to read? Like the stacks of *Road Warrior* that are more than ten years old?"

He concedes, "Yeah, I guess I should get around to that...sometime." He pours himself another bowl of Wheaties.

You press on, "And how about the 20 car batteries

that are in the garage from the time you wanted to convert the VW to an electric car?"

He nods, "Oh, yeah. I guess most of those batteries are dead by now. Or leaking acid. I should dispose of them...somehow."

You brighten, "Great! You can start this afternoon!"

He objects, "But...but....[deep sigh]...Okay."

"And while you're at it, you can dispose of your old sweaty high-school football jersey!"

"No!" He slams down his spoon. "Now you've gone *too far!* I scored the winning touchdown with that jersey. I've preserved it for thirteen years, and I'm not giving it up now!"

You've gotten him to make one move after another, but now you've just discovered his immediate limit.

So you relent: "That's okay, we can keep the sweaty football jersey for now. But...can we wash it?"

He sighs, "Okay, I guess so."

The trick to testing by pushing is: you've got to back away once you reach the other person's immediate limit. If you keep pushing and irritate them, you may alienate them entirely.

Is there a way to sense when you're approaching someone's immediate limit? Is there a method to indicate when you're getting close, so you don't push too far? There is.

Monitoring conversational cues. These are signals that people send to indicate what they are prepared to do for you and when you are reaching their immediate limit. When your husband yells, "Now you've gone

too far!" that is a pretty obvious conversational cue that
you have reached his limit.

But people send conversational cues not only by the
words they say but also by the way they say them—
their tone of voice, the words they choose to emphasize, their body language, how fast they speak, and
how loudly. Any of these elements can convey the
other person's willingness to do what you want.

Once you become aware of conversational cues, you
realize that our interactions are filled with them. People are constantly sending signals about what they are
willing to do. You'll recognize a number of such cues
in this example:

It's 4 p.m. Susan is sitting at her desk poring over
papers. Her co-worker, Tim, walks up to her. He
says, "I just finished preparing this report. Can you
give me your comments on it?"

She looks up. "I'm sorry, Tim, I'm swamped right
now. I've got this analysis to write."

He presses, "Well, I have to present this report tomorrow morning and I could *really* use your help."

Susan waves at the papers on her desk. "Look, I'd
like to help you. But I am really busy right now."

He insists: "Aw, come on. Can't you find five
minutes for me?"

She repeats: "I'm sorry, it's just not a good time."

So he tries, "Look, I wouldn't bother you except for
that thing you said in the meeting the other day about
how we needed to work together as a team."

She sighs, "Oh, that's right. I did say that, didn't I?"

He smiles. "Yes, you did."

Look at all the conversational cues in this short dialogue. Susan sent a lot of cues initially that she was not willing to do what Tim wanted. She said, "I'm sorry...I'm swamped," and she repeated that she was really busy. But then her immediate limit suddenly changed. It expanded. She realized, "Oops! I *did* make that comment about teamwork! If I don't follow through now, he'll never let me forget it!" She signaled this change, perhaps unconsciously, with another conversational cue—sighing and admitting, "I did say that, didn't I?"

This is a *strategic moment*—the moment when the other person becomes more willing or able to do what you want.

But, like most of us, Tim did not know he should be looking for a conversational cue or a strategic moment. If he had known, he could have seized the moment by reinforcing her more cooperative mood. He could have offered to help Susan with her project or to order dinner if they had to stay late.

As it was, Tim didn't even see the opening. He plowed ahead and kept pressuring her: "So how about if I just leave this report on your desk...." And she got exasperated: "Tim, I already told you, this is not a good time!"

Tim's talking got him nowhere because, as Susan told me later, he was "insensitive"—*un*strategic in his approach to her. Even when she signaled her position was softening, he failed to take the hint! And so, Tim lost the chance to get her cooperation. Like many strategic moments, this opportunity was fleeting. It quickly disappeared.

Susan's cue that her position was softening may seem subtle, but then so are many conversational cues. People don't always come right out and announce: "My position has changed!"

The more you get to know the other person's normal way of communicating, the more accurately you'll be able to interpret their conversational cues. The individual who appears to be yelling at you may not be upset; that may be their normal way of speaking. At the other extreme, someone with a more reserved communication style may raise their voice only slightly to signal they are out of patience and that you're at their immediate limit.

Learning to read other people's communication styles is vital because a lot of conversational cues are indirect.

Take, for instance, a typical labor negotiation. The union was asking for a 5% raise, management was offering 2%.

Then the union president thought aloud: "Even if I were to agree with you about wages, we'd still have to agree on the length of the contract—two years or three."

Fortunately, the management negotiator recognized this conversational cue, because it marked a strategic moment. The union president was hinting she might budge on wages—*if* management accepted a three-year contract. This is a common face-saving tactic: you hint that you might budge if they do; but if they refuse, you deny you were dropping a hint about budging; you reassert your original position and appear as strong as ever.

The management negotiator replied, "Well, a three-year deal might be a possibility...Let's see.."

People's attitudes and beliefs shift in the give-and-take of conversation, and often these shifts are accompanied by conversational cues. So get in the habit of watching for them. Clever kids look for a strategic moment when mom or dad is in a good mood before they ask a favor.

The more you observe someone's conversational cues, the more you'll become attuned to shifts in their immediate limit.

Use all three techniques. (Again, the three methods to estimate an immediate limit are: *examining their perceptions*, *testing by pushing*, and *monitoring conversational cues*.)

After you use one of these methods to gauge an immediate limit, check out your conclusion by using the other two approaches. If you develop similar estimates using different methods, you may be on the right track.

When you're gauging an immediate limit, remember: the best you can do is develop a good estimate. Treat it as a hypothesis that needs revision, not as an established fact. Be open to new evidence that refutes your theory.

You might have thought that your husband would

be willing to get rid of that sweaty football jersey. But because you are open to seeing that you might be wrong, you're able to recognize that you misjudged his immediate limit and you're able to adapt your strategy accordingly.

Be realistic, not optimistic

This philosophy runs counter to America's "can-do" spirit: if they say it can't be done, we'll find a way to do it.

This optimism can produce astonishing results. If we believe that nothing is impossible, we'll charge off to do it and sometimes we'll surprise everyone and succeed. The results can be so impressive, they can fool us into believing there are no limits, that people can do anything if only they truly want to.

I'm an optimistic person myself. As a negotiator, I delight in resolving problems that people think are impossible. But I'm under no illusions that it's realistic to expect anyone to do anything.

To make sure the move you're creating is realistic, you've got to identify the person's immediate limit.

In seminars I demonstrate this point by saying, "Pick the farthest place in the room that you'd like me to go in my next step. Anywhere at all." Inevitably someone picks a spot thirty feet across the room. I say, "Now here's the problem. I *cannot* go across the room in my next move. See my immediate limit?"

I stretch out my leg so everyone can see: at most I can go three feet in my next move.

"You could exhort me, you could cajole me, you could pressure me to go thirty feet in one leap across the room—and it wouldn't do any good, because it's beyond my ability. In fact, I might not even try because I can see it's absurd. So if you want me to go thirty feet across the room, don't try to make me do it in one move. Ask me to go three feet at first. Step by step, I'll be able to reach the thirty-foot mark."

Here the move is physical; in other situations, you'll want someone to make a mental move—like recognizing that a rent increase is long overdue.

Whether you want them to make a move that is physical or mental, what can you do if the move right now is unrealistic—as unrealistic as going to the thirty-foot mark? What if you want them to make a *big* move? These were the questions facing my girlfriend Naomi. The solution is to...

Break the problem apart

Call it male intuition, but I just knew that Naomi wanted me to propose to her. I knew because of certain hints that she would drop which were, in terms of size, comparable to a refrigerator. Examples:

"Hey, David! There's a movie on TV tonight where Billy Crystal falls in love and gets married. Doesn't that sound wonderful? In real life, I mean."

"Sure, let's order pizza! Now, we've got some decisions to make: do we want olives and mushrooms, when should we get married, do we want anchovies..."

"Oh, look at Mike and Sharon. They're so happy together. They're *married,* you know."

"Inasmuch as we could die in a car crash tomorrow, wouldn't you prefer to die *married,* with someone you love forever, instead of with someone you're casually dating?"

Through Naomi's subtle hints, gradually the point began to sink in that maybe we should get married. The problem was that getting married seemed like a *big* decision—one of life's biggest decisions, and I didn't want to rush it. As the months went by, Naomi, as you might expect, was getting a mite impatient.

Fortunately for me, she did not give up. Instead, she broke down the big decision about getting married into a series of smaller decisions: I'd have to decide with her whether to have kids, and if so, how many; I'd have to decide with her where we were going to settle down and whether we were going to rent or buy a home; I'd have to figure out with her what kind of wedding we would want to have.

Naomi reasoned, "After he dispenses with all the practical issues, the only remaining step will be to propose."

So over the next few weeks, Naomi brought up one topic at a time. She'd muse over dinner, "I realize you haven't proposed yet"—she'd preface all her musings by saying this—"but where do you think we should settle down?" We'd talk about that. Then a few days later, she'd mention, "I realize you haven't proposed yet, but do you think we should rent, or buy?"

Before I knew it, we'd begun planning the wedding.

By breaking things down and leading me through one issue at a time, she made me more comfortable with each aspect of getting married. It didn't seem like such a big step from singlehood anymore. Sure, it was still a significant commitment. But now, instead of seeming like a step into the great abyss, it seemed like a natural progression from a series of decisions I had already made—about the person, lifestyle, and values.

Gradually, the idea of getting married became more realistic to me. I could visualize it and become comfortable with it. Pretty soon it became almost comical that we had worked everything out, yet I hadn't proposed.

So I proposed.

Create one realistic move after another. When you subdivide a problem into manageable moves for the other person to make, an impossible goal can become realistic.

Look at what Abraham did when he was negotiating with the Lord. Let me suggest to you that this is not negotiating from a position of power. Let me suggest to you that this is the worst power disparity imaginable. Yet, even in this situation, the step-by-step approach succeeded.

Here's the challenge: The Lord has just revealed to Abraham that He plans to destroy the cities of Sodom and Gomorrah because they are wicked. Can Abraham, a mere human being, possibly persuade the Lord to change His plans?

You'll have to admit, the task sounds impossible. But open your Bible to Chapter 18 of the Book of Genesis and observe Abraham's strategy.

Abraham begins by asking, "Uh...are You going to destroy the righteous people with the wicked people? I mean, on the chance that there might be fifty righteous people in Sodom, would You destroy the whole city and not spare the town for those fifty righteous people? Because that's not like You—to kill the righteous with the wicked. Should not You, the Judge of all the earth, do right?"

Abraham is proposing a move that he would like the Lord to make. He's saying: How about saving the city if there are fifty righteous people? This move turns out to be within the Lord's immediate limit.

For the Lord replies, "If I find in Sodom fifty righteous people, then I will spare the whole place for their sakes."

This is quite an accomplishment for Abraham. But does he stop there? No. Just as Naomi kept presenting me with one realistic step after another, so Abraham keeps presenting the Lord with another step, then another.

Abraham prefaces his next request with humility: "Behold! I have taken it upon myself to speak to the Lord! Who am I but dust and ashes! Uh...now, about those fifty righteous people. On the chance that You can find only forty-five righteous people, on the chance that the city lacks five additional righteous people...will You destroy the city for lack of five people?"

And the Lord replies, "OK, Abraham, if I find forty-five righteous people, I will not destroy the city."

Abraham asks, "Uh...on the chance that there are only *forty* righteous people...?"

The Lord answers, "OK, Abraham, I will save the city for forty people."

Abraham says, "Oh, Lord, I hope You're not angry with me. It's just..uh...on the chance that there are only *thirty* righteous people??"

The Lord replies, "Yes, yes, I will save it for thirty."

Abraham asks, "Twenty?"

The Lord replies, "OK, Abraham, twenty."

Abraham says, "Oh, Lord, I really hope You're not angry with me now. I have only one last question. On the chance there are only *ten* righteous people?"

The Lord replies, "OK, OK, I will save it for ten."

And the Lord went on his way and Abraham returned unto his place.

If Abraham had asked the Lord initially to save Sodom for only ten people, the Lord might have refused. It might have been too big a step too soon—outside the Lord's immediate limit.

Abraham broke the problem apart. By leading the Lord to make one realistic move after another, Abraham convinces the Lord to save Sodom if there are only ten people worth saving. (Unfortunately, there are not, so the Lord wipes out Sodom and Gomorrah with fire and brimstone. But you can't blame Abraham for that. His approach succeeded. He persuaded the Almighty.)

The step-by-step approach doesn't work just in the Bible. It also works in business.

At one company, Marketing and Engineering were engaged in a corporate version of the Cold War. Marketing would complain, "You aren't designing it the way we want!" Engineering would reply, "Your expectations are unrealistic!" To make peace, Elaine, the Marketing director, called Bill, the Engineering manager, and suggested that the two departments get together for a seminar on teamwork.

Bill snapped, *"You're* the ones who have trouble working with *us. We* don't need lessons on teamwork!"

Elaine slammed down the phone. Then she called me. "It's so frustrating! I want to mend fences, and he's not even willing to meet! Can *you* get through to him?"

Good question. Bill loathed Marketing. I couldn't expect him to pay attention to me as a representative of Marketing. I'd have to get him to make a smaller move first. Before he would listen to me, he'd have to conclude that I was *worth* dealing with. Here was my strategy:

I called Bill and said, "I've been hired to teach the Marketing staff better ways of resolving conflicts. So I'd like to learn what mistakes Marketing routinely makes in dealing with your department."

Sure enough, he recited a *litany* of errors.

After a few minutes on the phone, I suggested, "There are too many problems here to discuss in one phone call. But I can meet at a time convenient for you." Bill agreed to meet, because he wanted to keep criticizing Marketing to somebody who might actually get them to change.

If I had suggested a face-to-face meeting initially, he would have refused. Why should he spend time with a stranger from Marketing who therefore would not be trustworthy? He'd think I'd been sent to harass him.

I wanted to allay his concerns. That's why I disclosed that I wanted to help Marketing improve. That established my credibility. *Then* I proposed a meeting.

I showed Bill an outline of the seminar that I was planning to teach to the Marketing department. Soon, he was critiquing the outline; we were working together. After several meetings, I suggested: "You've helped a lot designing this training; it would be nice if you could be there."

Again, one step at a time. First I asked him to help create the program, *then* I invited him to attend. Now his choice was whether to continue cooperating with someone he trusted, instead of whether to collaborate with the enemy.

Earlier, he had perceived that the Marketing director was trying to force a workshop on him. But he saw this new training as a way to help Marketing change. He was proud of it. Not only did Bill come, he asked the entire Engineering department to come.

At the workshop the two staffs began working together on the real issues between their departments. Gradually the feud dissolved, and Bill finally forgave Elaine for the time she embarrassed him in a staff meeting, five years ago, by accident.

You direct their anger
by creating their next move

Often when I tell this story to a seminar group, someone raises a hand and asks: "I don't get it. You asked
Bill to talk about Marketing's mistakes? Why did you
do that? Seems to me he was complaining enough.
Did you want to encourage him to complain?"

Yes, I did—because I was prepared to act on his
complaints. The more he complained, the more convinced he became that Marketing had to change. And
I was providing the only option to get Marketing to
change. So really, I was inviting him to talk himself
into cooperating with me.

Someone else's hand shoots up here: "But as you
pointed out yourself, a lot of times when you let someone vent, it only makes things *worse!*"

Absolutely. I was inviting Bill to vent, but I had
decided beforehand how to turn his energy toward a
constructive goal—the creation of the new workshop.

It *is* very risky to invite someone to vent if you don't
know how to deal with their anger once they release it.
Indeed, one purpose of creating the other person's
next move is to direct their negative feelings toward a
constructive target, or at least toward a harmless target.
That's how you begin to defuse someone's anger.

Begin to defuse?

That's right: human beings, like many complex ex-
plosive devices, often cannot be defused in one move.

Don't try to solve
too big a problem at once

Why did our strategy succeed in a cease fire between these two departments?

Because we broke the problem apart. We kept asking ourselves: "What can we get Bill to do *now?*" The first move was for him to discuss his problems with Marketing. The second move was for him to agree to meet. The third move was for him to work on the training outline with me. One step at a time, each move within his immediate limit.

Why did Bill refuse to get together for a workshop at the beginning? Because he wasn't ready.

It was too big a step, too soon. Elaine, the Marketing director, was focusing on her ultimate goal— cooperation—and pushing for it right away, without considering whether it was realistic.

It's tempting in a dispute to try to come up with the brilliant answer that will settle the whole problem all at once. Then you present it to the other side. That's what Elaine was doing by saying, "Let's hold a joint training!"

That's like walking up to a stranger and saying, "Marry me." There are smaller steps required before you reach that point (at least in mainstream US culture). Persuasion is like courtship. You've got to lead the person one step at a time. And you can't expect to resolve a complex issue all at once, in a master stroke.

Bill, the Engineering director, did not take one single action that in itself resolved the issue. We invited him to make a series of moves, each one building on the preceding one, to culminate in a satisfactory outcome.

By the way, when you're trying to resolve a big issue, don't imply that the whole problem would go away if only the person made one small move toward resolving it. (Imagine how upset your husband would be if he finally threw away his stacks of *Road Warrior* magazines to satisfy you about cleaning up the garage, only to find that you were still pestering him to get rid of his other junk there.)

Tips for creating their next move

Conventional wisdom:	Strategic communication:
Think, "What's the biggest move *I want* them to make?"	Think, "What's the biggest move *they are willing* to make?"
Ask for everything, or you certainly won't receive it.	Don't ask for too much, or they may refuse to give anything.
If time is short, push for everything now.	Regardless of time pressure, pursue only what you can get now.
Focus on their "bottom line" (ultimate limit).	Determine the other person's *immediate limit.*

What if you don't have time to go step by step?

Surprise! Proceeding incrementally is the *fastest* way to get what you want. The slowest way is to push for too much at once. That's when the other person gets defensive, locks up and refuses to budge—as the Engineering director did initially.

But if each move you invite them to make is easy for them, you'll make progress quickly.

Don't plan all your steps at once

Even when you know exactly where you want to lead the other person, it's best at the outset *not* to develop every single step that you will take.

Dealing with people is not like playing chess, where you can develop an intricate plan many steps ahead. A chess piece is simpler than your average human being. Its movement is much more restricted. A bishop can move only diagonally. A rook can move only in a line. A king can normally move only one square.

Whereas a human being is capable of careening all over the board, every which way.

Psychologists have shown that you can predict how a human being will respond in many situations. It is often possible to predict a human being's next move. It is far more difficult to predict now what a human being's second, third, and fourth moves will be.

A human being is also more finicky than a chess piece. You can control a chess piece. You must persuade a human being: a human being must *decide* to do what you want. A chess piece never says no. A human being often says no. Thus, when you're dealing with a human being, you continually have to revise your plan to adapt to changing circumstances.

One of the worst things you can do is to develop at the outset every step you will take and then to follow that plan like a script.

When I was in college, I had a roommate named Freddie who was so painfully afraid of women that he created a rigid plan for going out on dates:

1. Show up with roses,
2. Hold her hand, and
3. Kiss her.

I remember after one date Freddie came back to the room with a black eye. He told me that the first step (the roses) had gone well. However, his date was not ready for the second step (holding hands). But Freddie followed his plan and kept taking her hand anyway. Then he tried to execute step three.

This explained the black eye.

Freddie wanted to plan all his steps in advance because, like many of us in an uncomfortable situation, he was anxious. He didn't want to blow it. He was nervous about how the other person would respond.

Freddie got it backwards.

The less certain you are about how someone will behave, the more closely you need to pay attention to them, instead of ignoring them and following your own script. Instead of focusing on what he would do, Freddie should have considered what *she* was emotionally ready and willing to do.

Especially in a delicate situation, you need to tune in to the person's immediate limit and decide what to do in response to it. Your greatest asset is responsiveness,

not rigidity. You've got to respond to the situation as it unfolds. You don't know whether a series of steps you create at the outset will be constructive later when you execute them.

So for heaven's sake, don't plan all the steps of your strategy at once in advance.

Instead, *create only one move right now for the other person to make.* Then see whether they make it. What if they don't?

You don't have to dig in

If the other person balks, you don't have to insist on their making that particular move. You can get creative and invent another one, instead. You don't have to declare: "It's my way or no way!"

The move that you create is one *option* about what they *could* do. It is not a *command* about what they *must* do.

Freddie missed this distinction. When his date did not do what he wanted, he thought he had to insist that she do it anyway. He kept trying to impose his agenda on her. He didn't know what else to do.

He was trying to control the other person.

Big mistake.

It is impossible for you to *dictate* the other person's next move. You can develop an option for them to take. *They* must *decide* whether to take it. They alone have the power to say yes or no.

If they say no, re-examine their immediate limit to decide what move *would* be realistic for them to make.

BUT YOUR JOB ISN'T OVER THEN. After you develop a realistic move for them to make, you've still got to entice them to make it. Just because the other person is willing or able to do something does not mean they will do it on their own. Chances are, you'll have to approach them first. And the way you approach them is critical. It makes the difference between persuading them and alienating them.

How can you design an approach that entices someone to do what you want?

That's the focus of the next chapter.

❖❖ *Key points for applying strategic step #2:* **Create the other person's next move**

1. Remember: The next move *you* should make depends on the next move you want the *other* person to make. First determine what you want *them* to do.

2. Approach the right person—someone who is *influential* enough to help you get what you want, and *receptive* enough to listen to you.

3. Don't focus on the other person's "bottom line"— the most they might do for you ultimately. Focus on their *immediate limit*—the most they are willing and able to do for you right now.

4. Use all three techniques for uncovering someone's immediate limit:
   • examining their perceptions,

- testing by pushing, and
- monitoring conversational cues.

5. If you want the person to make a big move that right now is unrealistic, break the problem apart. Invite them to make a smaller move; then follow up with another, and another.

6. Don't develop at the outset all the steps you will take and then follow them like a script. The steps you develop now may turn out to be counterproductive later when you execute them. *Create only one move right now for the other person to make.*

Use their own perceptions to convince them

You want to tell them your point of view, but they insist on their own perspective. You might be tempted to tell them they're wrong, that they should change their mind, that they should see things your way. There is a better approach.

The prevailing view about how to persuade someone is that you've got to be a great communicator. Your personality has to be so charming and your arguments have to be so polished that you win over the other side.

The *Wall Street Journal* did a profile of chief executive officers (CEOs) who had lost their jobs after high-profile failures, only to be rehired as top executives someplace else. Take the example of Frank Lorenzo. He was CEO of Eastern Airlines. They went bankrupt. He was CEO of Continental Airlines. They went bankrupt. So what happened to Lorenzo?

According to the *Journal,* he got investors to give him millions to start a third airline.

Bill Agee was CEO of Bendix. His reported big failure there was his attempt to take over Martin Marietta Corporation. As the *Journal* tells the story, Martin Marietta fought back, and when all the fighting was over, Bendix as an independent corporation ceased to exist. (It became part of a company now known as AlliedSignal Inc.) Agee was out of a job.

But only temporarily. He became CEO of Morrison Knudsen.

The *Journal* asked people who knew these CEOs: What is their secret? How do they bounce back?

Again and again, their colleagues replied: He had such a winning personality. Such charisma. Such enthusiasm. He was so articulate. So charming.

One person said of Bill Agee: "He can convince you that white is black."

This magic ability to captivate people reminds me of the famous TV commercial for EF Hutton. People are noisily bustling about, when suddenly...*silence*. Everyone stands still. The announcer explains: "When EF Hutton talks, people listen."

However, if your personal experience is like mine, namely that when you speak, people don't wait for your next word, that in fact they interrupt you, walk away, or even pick up the phone to talk to *someone else*...well, then, this chapter is for you.

There are people who are born with charisma, and then there are the rest of us. The popular notion is that the rest of us are out of luck, because the only way to persuade people is to be a smooth talker.

Nonsense.

You can influence people by developing sound strategy. You don't have to be like the master hypnotist Svengali. And you don't need to try to change your personality to become the "great communicator" who bowls over the other person.

But you do need to set aside a lot of folk wisdom about how to work with people.

"What they think is their problem"

We are taught that persuading someone is like pouring water into an empty glass. Their mind is the empty glass, and your knowledge is the water that you are pouring into their mind.

Whatever they believe now is irrelevant. Your ideas are right, so why should you care what they think? You are going to change their mind, anyway.

This was the attitude of the captain of the chain gang in *Cool Hand Luke*. Paul Newman's rebellious thinking did not matter. Strother Martin looks at Newman's crumpled body on the floor and insists, "You're gonna get your mind *right*. And I mean: *right*."

This philosophy reminds me of the wisecrack, "When I want your opinion, I'll give it to you."

Offensive as it is, this mindset is deeply ingrained in us. It may even be so deeply ingrained that we cannot see it's there. The axiom is that persuading someone involves attacking their beliefs with your own.

How ingrained is this axiom? Well, if you look in the dictionary under "persuade," the first four words in Webster's are "to move by argument."

Further, whenever there's a gap between their position and ours, and they are hopelessly stubborn, the tendency is to think, "How can we get *them* to be more open-minded? Less emotional? More reasonable? More willing to compromise?"

These are all ways of saying we want them to leave their position and come over to ours. We want *them* to bridge the gap. We want *them* to change.

In other words, we don't care what they think now. The adage is, "What they think is their problem." We want them to see things our way.

But how likely is that to happen?

People believe their own perceptions

How likely is the other person to come over to your way of thinking? By definition, not very likely at all, if the other person is stubborn. (Even after all those beatings, Paul Newman's character still defied the captain.)

If the other person has a belief that conflicts with yours, do you really think they'll set aside their own belief to accept yours? Unlikely. Whose belief will they accept?

Their own, naturally. People find their own perceptions the most convincing.

What they think is their problem? Hardly. It's your problem, too, if you're trying to persuade them. People decide what to do based on *their* perceptions, not yours.

Recall the feud between the heads of Marketing and Engineering. At first, Elaine, the Marketing boss, suggested to Bill, the Engineering manager, that the staffs of both departments get together for a seminar on teamwork. She was proceeding on the assumption that both staffs needed to improve.

But that was her assumption, not his.

He assumed *her* staff was the problem, so he said no.

I went back to Bill and built on this perception of his. I said to him, "I'd like to learn what mistakes Marketing routinely makes in dealing with you." Then he cooperated.

Your approach to persuade someone should be based on *their* perceptions, not your own. The other person's beliefs should dictate your strategy.

Conventional wisdom says the reverse. The accepted wisdom is that your strategy should dictate their beliefs. After all, the logic goes, the whole point of persuasion is to change the other person's mind.

Thus, a typical approach is to tell someone, *"You're wrong. You've got to change."* But if someone says that to you, do you feel like cooperating? Probably not. When human beings come under attack, what's their natural response?

To fight back and defend themselves.

So don't automatically go into a meeting blasting the other person's point of view. Don't automatically attempt to change their mind. As a rule, avoid challenging their perceptions with your own. You are bound to produce resistance.

I could not have persuaded the Engineering manager by articulating *my* belief that he should cooperate. He thought he shouldn't, so he would have said no. To get him to cooperate, I had to start with *his* perspective that Marketing was wrong.

You see, the way we've been taught to persuade someone is exactly backwards. We should not try to make the other person hold the same views that we do. Often, that's not realistic. We cannot expect the other person to believe *our* perceptions.

We should persuade them using *theirs*.

Should you care what they think?

Conventional wisdom says no:	Strategic communication says yes:
What they think is their problem.	Their thinking is precisely *your* problem.
You want them to act on *your* ideas, not theirs.	They act on *their own* perceptions, not yours.
Their existing beliefs do not matter.	Their perceptions determine whether they say yes or no.
Your strategy should dictate their beliefs.	Their beliefs should dictate your strategy.

Perceptions are hidden motivators

Your perception is your picture of reality, filtered by your biases and interpretations—your ego, vanity, fear, desire, and other emotions. It's common knowledge that human beings view the world through foggy glasses. Yet we tend to forget that our own vision is cloudy. We tend to accept our view of reality as reality itself.

For instance, let's say you're a manager and you notice that your employee is working fifteen-hour days to finish a project on time. What would you think about that? Perhaps that he's putting out tremendous effort and that he deserves to be rewarded. Perhaps a bonus would be in order.

Or...you might assume that someone who's putting in fifteen hours a day is incompetent. You hired him

to do the work in eight hours, and something's wrong if he's not able to accomplish it. A bonus? Hah! You'd have to have a serious talk with him about why he can't accomplish the task in the time allotted.

Your perception of your employee's long hours determines whether you laud him or chastise him.

But regardless of what you do, you probably won't realize that your perception motivated you to do it. You won't think, "I'm giving him a bonus because of my view of him." You'll think, "I'm giving him a bonus because he deserves it." You'll think you were responding solely to your employee, not to your own perception.

Our perceptions motivate us without our realizing it. That's why we don't recognize how powerful they are. But our perceptions are fundamental motivators of our behavior.

This is especially true when it comes to dating.

Have you ever thought about how you decide whom to try to go out with? Researchers from the University of Minnesota and the University of Wisconsin did a study about this, and they found you are not most likely to ask out someone who's absolutely stunning. You are most likely to ask out someone who's about as attractive as you are. Can you guess the researchers' explanation?

You think the gorgeous person would reject you. This perception convinces you to set your sights lower. When will you change and start asking out people who are better-looking?

Your behavior will change when your perception changes. I know this from my own dating experience. For years, I thought that nobody attractive would want to go out with me, so I didn't bother asking. Then one day in college, a very cute co-ed named Jennifer actually expressed interest in me. I could not believe this was happening. (Unfortunately, this was the blonde I told you about, with whom I blundered by commenting that I was not especially attracted to blondes.) Jennifer changed the way I looked at dating. Suddenly I realized, "If *she* would go out with me, maybe other attractive women would, too." Gradually I became less bashful about asking out desirable women until finally I asked out Naomi.

Not just in the land of dating but in all kinds of settings, studies show that people decide what to do based on their perceptions. A UCLA researcher went into an elementary school and gave kids a puzzle to do. She gave them so little time to do it, she knew they would fail. When they did fail, she told some of the kids, "I'm angry with you." She told others, "I feel sorry for you."

Now, consider the kids at whom she got angry. What do you suppose they thought about *why* she got mad?

They assumed she was expecting them to do better. They inferred they were smart and weren't trying.

Now consider the kids to whom she expressed pity. What do you suppose *they* thought? They thought they weren't good at doing puzzles like this.

Then she gave all the kids another puzzle. Sure enough, the kids who perceived they had low ability gave up sooner. The kids who inferred they were smarter persisted longer.

So: our perceptions determine whether we strive toward a goal, how hard we strive, and even what goal we set.

If you want to get someone to do something, start by examining their perceptions.

How do you uncover someone's perceptions?

Let's take a typical problem: your landlady is dragging her feet about fixing your leaky roof, and you want to figure out why. Whenever you want to identify someone's perceptions, you can use seven techniques:

1. Consider: Why should they? And why shouldn't they? One way to discover what the other person is thinking is to focus on the move you want them to make (in this case, fixing the roof) and to ask yourself two simple questions: From their perspective, *why should they?* And *why shouldn't they?*

Their rationale doesn't have to be logical. Their rationale is *their* thinking. It may not be logical at all.

A common mistake is to put yourself in your landlady's shoes and imagine what perceptions you would have if you were in her place. Even if you were a landlady, you would not necessarily think the way she does. You might want to fix that leaky roof right away.

Focus on how *she* sees her decision. Why does *she*

think she should fix the roof? And why does *she* think she shouldn't?

2. Think about what they've said. To learn what's on her mind, reflect on what she herself has already told you. Suppose she's said, "Why should I bother making repairs? You're leaving in a few months anyway." Now you know why she's refusing to act.

3. Look for patterns in their behavior. Suppose she keeps telling you, "I promise to fix the roof!" but never does anything. If her actions and words don't match, ask yourself what possible perception of hers would explain the discrepancy.

Perhaps she thinks that if she puts you off long enough, you'll give up.

Reflect on how she's responded to your calls for help in the past. If in the last seven years she has never, ever returned any of your phone calls and has always procrastinated when you have raised issues, these behavior patterns may just possibly be clues that she has a perception that you are not worth her attention.

4. Ask them what they're thinking. "Can you tell me what you see as the major obstacle to fixing the leak?" If she's open with you, you may get an earful. It may turn out she is procrastinating because she's still mad at you for the time you drove over her petunias with the moving van.

5. Get advice from people who know them. If your landlady won't give you straight answers about what she's thinking, and if you're up for doing some

extra homework, consider: Who else would know
what's on her mind? A mutual friend? A colleague of
hers? Someone of her culture? To get a landlady's
perspective, try talking to a fellow landlady.

Also consult people who've dealt with this individual
on similar issues. You're not the first to talk to her
about repairs. Get information from others who
have—fellow tenants. What did they discover about
her beliefs and attitudes?

A cautionary note: Approach people you can trust to
keep your inquiry confidential. If they tell your landlady that you're asking about her, she may get nervous
about your intentions. She may not realize that you're
simply trying to learn her point of view.

6. Look behind one perception to find another.
One technique to identify their deep-seated perceptions is to start with an obvious belief of theirs and ask
yourself what lies behind it. Let's say your landlady's
obvious belief is that she bears no responsibility for
fixing the roof. What lies behind that conclusion?
What leads her to think it is correct?

When you dig, you may find a deeper, underlying
perception. She may think she bears no responsibility
because a neighbor told her you held a wild dance
party on the roof, in violation of the big sign that says,
"DO NOT GO ON ROOF."

7. Brainstorm possible perceptions. Make a list of
all the beliefs and attitudes she might possibly have
about the roof issue. Then go through and weed out
the perceptions that are clearly out of character for her.

What if their beliefs are irrational?

There is a danger that as you come to understand the other's perceptions, you will be repulsed by them or think they are stupid. The more you learn about the other person, the more you may dislike them.

(Of course, the more they learn about *you*, the more they may dislike *you*. That's precisely why you should refrain from unthinkingly blurting out your own beliefs. Recall my blunder with Jennifer, the blonde co-ed to whom I communicated my belief that blondes were not especially attractive.) Better understanding can drive people further apart.

If the person's perceptions make no sense, the temptation is to disregard them. You figure, "Why should I pay attention to their stupid beliefs?" That's a big mistake. The other person will act on them anyway, because: *people believe their own perceptions.*

Your idea of reality is as accurate to you as what you touch and smell. If you pass a panhandler on the street who looks like he hasn't shaved in a week and you have the thought, "He's a drunk," that view of him is as accurate to you as the sight of the stubble on his chin.

Of course, your assumption *may* be objectively true: the man *may* be a drunk. If you give him money, he *may* use it to buy booze. But whether or not your interpretation is accurate, you *presume* that it is. And so, regardless of its accuracy, your perception determines what you're willing to do for him; it determines your immediate limit. (Remember, your immediate limit is the most that you are willing and able to do for someone right now.) If you think, "Poor guy just lost his job and needs a few bucks for a meal," your immediate limit is greater; you may be willing to give him some money.

Again: Our perceptions determine our behavior regardless of whether they are accurate. In this respect, a person's perception of reality is more important than reality itself. I used to be a broadcast journalist. On one story, I went inside a prison cell to interview a murderer named Willis James Crawford, whose case had made national headlines. Crawford had been working on his Ph.D. in physics at Stanford University, when one day he walked into his professor's office, hit him on the head with a hammer, and killed him.

I asked Crawford, "Why did you do it?"

He told me he wanted to protest the way Stanford treats its graduate students—luring them with the hope of a Stanford degree and then allegedly leaving them to toil for years in frustration, with insufficient help from their professors. This is a complaint among graduate students at many universities, and often it's true.

But I asked Crawford, "Why murder? Why did you choose to *kill* the professor to make your point?"

Here came the most fascinating part of the interview. He listed alternatives he had considered: "I considered taking it to the alumni, I considered agitating with the students, I considered vandalism, I considered politics..." And he proceeded to tell me why an action other than murder would not have gotten his point across effectively.

Objectively, did he have an alternative to murder? Could he have protested another way? Does it matter? The professor is dead because Crawford *believed* alternative action would not be as effective.

His belief determined his action. Objective reality about his options did not drive him to kill. His perception drove him to kill. That's how powerful our perceptions are. People don't make decisions based on a purely objective reality. They make decisions based on *their view* of reality—their perceptions.

Make their perceptions your foundation

Whether you agree with their perceptions makes no difference. You should avoid fighting them.

In fact, you should proceed on the basis of them.

When you're trying to get someone to do what you want, the easiest way is not to try to change their beliefs. That can be impossible. The easiest way is to get them to do what you want *because* of their beliefs.

By harnessing their perceptions, you can turn *no* into *yes*. I once worked at a company where the purchasing manager was, well, difficult to work with. Every third purchasing request that he received, he would stamp *Disapproved*. It didn't matter whether you had called 17 zillion stores and gotten the absolutely rock-bottom certifiably lowest price. This man would delight in using the power of his position to make you go back and get a lower price. If you could not get a better price, he would not approve your request.

By withholding his approval arbitrarily, he succeeded in making himself feel important at your expense. And I had to deal with him.

I wanted to get a computer from a particular store that offered great service. It also happened to have the best price. But I knew that if I walked into this bureaucrat's office with three bids, and if on that day he happened to feel like throwing his weight around, he would stamp my request *Disapproved.*

My first thought was to submit a purchasing request to buy the computer from a store with lousy service and high prices; then he would say no because of the price, and I could return with a lower price from the store I really wanted.

The problem was, if he happened to be in a reasonable mood, he might actually say yes to the high-priced store, and then I would be stuck dealing with a store with lousy service—and it would cost my company more money!

How could I deal with a man so egotistical? So irrational? What could I do?

Absolutely nothing. At least, that was my initial conclusion. But then I stopped to consider his perceptions. I thought about my purchasing request from *his* perspective. I asked myself, "From his point of view, why *should* he let me buy the computer? Why *shouldn't* he?"

I knew why he shouldn't. He hadn't pushed me around yet. No matter that I had already found the best price. He had a perception that I didn't deserve to get what I wanted until he had turned me down, made me call 25,000 more stores, and forced me to come back to him pleadingly on bended knee. Until he had played his power game, he would say no.

Now, how could I turn that reason to say no into a reason to say yes?

(One of the benefits of asking, "Why shouldn't they?" is that you can anticipate their objections and plan how to resolve them.) I mused, "He believes that he *shouldn't* approve my request if he *hasn't* pushed me to get the best price. Therefore...he probably has another perception—that he *should* approve my request if he *has* pushed me to get the best price."

I walked into his office, laid all three bids on his desk, and announced, "You were right. I could get it cheaper!"

He grumbled, "See? I told you so!" and stamped it *Approved.*

In fact, this was the first time I had approached him about buying this computer. But he was so accustomed to being a jerk and saying no indiscriminately, he probably figured that he had said no to me, too. He figured that I was coming back to him after finding the best price.

In fact, I *was* coming to him after finding the best price. In fact, his reputation for being moody and capricious *had* prompted me to make double-sure I had gotten the best deal for the company.

Since he had a perception that he had to push people around, and since I was telling him that he had already pushed me to get the best price, naturally he was motivated to say yes.

Should you try to change *them*—or your approach?

Conventional wisdom:	Strategic communication:
When they're stubborn, tell them to change.	When they won't budge, change your approach.
Don't listen to their stupid point of view.	Pay attention to what they think.
Make them see that you are right.	See why they think that they are right.
Get them to say yes by attacking their beliefs.	Get them to say yes *because* of their beliefs.

What if you can't say what you want?

The Rolling Stones lamented, "You can't always get what you want," but sometimes there's an even more basic difficulty. Sometimes, you can't even *say* what you want—because if you do, you know that the other person will do exactly the opposite. For whatever reason, they're biased against you or they want to make life tough for you.

In those cases, you've got to lead the other person to make a move without your suggesting it.

My student Rich did just that. He was a computer expert for a large consulting firm. His boss had flown across the country for a meeting and, upon landing, had come down with the flu. So she called Rich and said, "I need you to fly out here and substitute for me at the meeting tomorrow morning." Well, tomorrow happened to be Rich's wedding anniversary. But Rich knew the company's view about that: "If it's personal, it doesn't matter. All that matters is the bottom line."

Of course, he would have preferred that his boss postpone the meeting. But he couldn't suggest that, because then he would be putting his needs ahead of the company's. So his dilemma was: how could he get her to reschedule, without his suggesting it?

He examined his boss' perceptions. In her mind, why should she reschedule—and why shouldn't she?

He knew her first consideration would be money. She was a cheapskate. She made a fuss about paying too much for anything. She made a fuss when he bought *paper clips* she thought were too expensive. She believed money was all important. He thought to himself, "How can I build on that perception?"
Well for starters, he decided not even to mention his anniversary. Instead, he called his travel agent. Then he called his boss: "The travel agent says I'm going to have to take a red-eye flight, fly eleven hours overnight, through three airports—but I know this meeting is important to you and you can depend on me to be there. I just need your authorization to purchase the plane ticket. The least expensive coast-to-coast plane fare with no advance notice is...$1,875."

Right then his boss decided to reschedule the meeting.

Of course, this had been Rich's idea all along, but it

was much better for him not to say so. His boss' belief in saving money led her inevitably to the idea of canceling the trip.

So to get what you want, you don't always have to make a request. If you do a good job of building on the other person's perception, you can rely on them to draw the conclusion you want.

Your idea must fit with theirs

Why did Rich's boss choose to reschedule the meeting? Because she believed in saving money. The idea of canceling the trip meshed with her belief in saving money.

For the other person to say yes, they've got to see that your request fits with their existing beliefs.

Remember, whenever someone hears a new idea, they compare it to their existing perceptions to see whether it makes sense. If your idea fits, they accept it. If not, they reject it.

Let's say the other person believes they can't trust you and that you go up to them and suggest, "Let's put the past behind us and trust each other"—a standard peace overture. Consider what happens in the other person's mind. The other person compares your suggestion—"Trust me"—with what they know about you, namely that you're not trustworthy.

Hence, they say no.

Does that mean you're defeated? Certainly not. Whenever someone says no, consider: What perception of theirs is preventing them from doing what you want? What belief, attitude, or interpretation of theirs is standing in your way? Perhaps you can turn this perception to your advantage.

If someone thinks I'm untrustworthy, I sometimes reply, "I don't expect you to trust me! You shouldn't sign an agreement unless you're convinced it's good for you." Here I'm clarifying. I'm not asking them to trust me. I'm making a different request—that they evaluate whether the outcome is good for them.

If I'm successful, they think: "He's asking me to judge whether this agreement meets my needs? That's no problem. I believe in doing that anyway!" They see that what I want is consistent with what they already believe.

Hence, they say yes.

Anytime you've gotten someone to say yes, you've succeeded because they have seen that your request is consistent with their beliefs. They have compared your request to their beliefs and concluded, "There's a match!"

Behind every success of yours lies a perception of theirs.

Select which perception you will build on

When I was going to elementary school, there were three fourth-grade teachers, and my mother wanted to make sure I got the best one. So she asked the principal for permission to observe all three teachers. He said, "OK, but it won't make any difference. Our policy is to assign the children ourselves."

Mom visited the classrooms and found that Mrs. Olexo was by far the best teacher. But how could Mom be sure I got Mrs. Olexo? The principal believed that parents should not pick teachers. If she had simply asked him to put me in Mrs. Olexo's class, he would have reiterated his policy.

Simply communicating her preference would not have sufficed. She had to think more about his perceptions. She thought, "From his perspective, why should he—and why shouldn't he—let me pick the teacher?"

Well, he *shouldn't* let her pick the teacher because he would think that he could choose better than she could. And honoring her request would be a hassle. He'd believe that as a busy principal, he should... *minimize hassles.*

Aha! That was the perception Mom decided to focus on. She said to him: "Let me tell you something about David. He can be a wonderful kid, or he can be a terrible kid. How he behaves depends on the teacher. Now, I can tell you that Mrs. Olexo has the touch. With her, he will be wonderful. With either of the other two teachers, he will be terrible. So: he will be happier, I will be happier, and *you* will be happier if he is in Mrs. Olexo's class."

I got into Mrs. Olexo's class without any trouble. (This was the approach Mom used to get me the right teacher throughout my elementary school years.)

Sure, the principal had a belief that parents should not pick teachers. Mom convinced him, anyway, because she built on an even more powerful perception of his—his belief that he should minimize hassles. She got him to envision a screaming fourth grader, and the image was not appealing. She got the principal to see that her request for Mrs. Olexo fit with his perception that he should minimize hassles.

Moral: Any particular human being is motivated by a lot of beliefs. You can choose which one you want to draw on. If the other person is operating from a perception that is unfavorable to you, don't immediately get discouraged. Ask yourself what other perceptions they have.

Fight one of their perceptions with another

Fresh out of college, I had to contend with the typical negative perception about people my age: I was too young to know anything. Nobody would take me seriously.

But because I knew what they were thinking, I could do something about it.

Of course, I could not openly say, "I want respect!" That would have reinforced the wrong perception. People would have thought, "Impatient kid! He'll get respect when he's earned it!" ("I want respect!" would have worked about as well as "Trust me!" Asking them for it would not have inspired them to give it.)

Instead, I started wearing suits. Because, as silly as it sounds, a lot of us think, "Person in suit! This individual must have something important to say!"

Their overriding perception about my suit was more persuasive to them than their bias against my age.

It can be very difficult to fight someone's perception. If you must do it, get some help—from the other person. Arm yourself with an *overriding perception*, a belief of theirs that is more persuasive to them than the unfavorable perception you wish to challenge.

I used an overriding perception early in my relationship with Naomi when we had had a big fight and neither of us was sure the relationship was going to last. She suggested getting together for a walk on the beach. She told me later that she came to the beach thinking, "This is probably the end. He doesn't care about me."

But I figured she was also thinking, "I want this relationship to last—*if* he shows me that he cares about me." Fortunately for me, this was an overriding perception. And to tap it, I did something that was, well, hardly original.

I showed up with a rose. But then, originality isn't what counts; it's the result that matters. The result was a scene from Hallmark. She threw her arms around me and we began crying—which made us both determined to work things out because we cared so much about each other.

OH, AND ON THE SUBJECT OF ROMANCE:

It is not easy to get mutant worms to make love.

You may not have considered this issue before, but Naomi has, because she is a *scientist* and it is her *job* to spend hours in the laboratory, getting mutant worms to make love, so they will give birth to baby mutant worms, who will contain exact copies of the parents' genes—which is Naomi's goal.

She works at cloning genes. To do that, you've got to get these mutant worms to make love.

This is not always as easy as you might think.

Naomi reports that while you can encourage the mutant worms to mate, they do not always do it. They are not always, shall we say, in the mood. Naomi has tried a lot of things to get them in the mood. She has talked to them. She has brought them chocolates. She has played a violin. She has even tried a rose.

But these worms are so stupid that even when they get in the mood, they do not always succeed at mating. This is because the worms will try to mate with anything they bump into, even if that thing is their own tail.

The point is: science takes a long time, and it is unpredictable. This is a maxim of worm work. Naomi once tried for *six months* to clone the gene of a particular worm, and when she wasn't having any luck, her boss came to her and pronounced: "Naomi, this is taking too long."

Naomi sighed, "I agree."

Her boss said firmly, "Naomi, I'd like you to work hard and finish this project in the next month!"

Naomi protested, "It's not up to *me!* It's up to the *worms!* The worms haven't cooperated for six months! How do you expect them to cooperate in thirty days?"

Her boss replied hopefully, with the manager's refrain: "Oh, if you try hard, I'm sure you can do it."

That was her boss' perception. It was a ridiculous perception, and she was tempted to say so. But rather than start an argument, Naomi took a deep breath and looked for another perception of his to focus on.

She pondered her boss' statement that if only she tried hard, she could succeed. She asked herself, "Why does he believe that? He knows I've been working hard for six months!"

That's when Naomi realized: her boss *wanted* to believe the cloning was easy. He didn't want to admit that this six-month project was a failure. He preferred to perceive that the task could easily be accomplished.

That was the perception Naomi chose to address.

The next time they discussed the gene cloning and her boss urged Naomi to "try harder," Naomi smiled sweetly, "It would be nice to think that the problem until now has been lack of effort, because then the solution would be simple: I'd work harder, and the project would get finished.

"But we both know the real problem is that science is unpredictable. Despite your best efforts, things always take longer than you expect. That's why we're in the present situation. And that's why we'll continue to be in this predicament until we bring this project to a close."

What did Naomi do here?

She was frustrated with her boss' perception that all she had to do was "try harder." So she looked behind that perception to find another. *Why* did he believe that trying harder would work? Because he wanted to perceive: "the task is easy."

She then challenged the notion that "the task is easy" with an overriding perception—"science is unpredictable." Her boss so strongly believed that "science is unpredictable," he realized that maybe the task was not so easy, after all.

He agreed to abandon the project.

How do you find an overriding perception?

An overriding perception has two components:
- It can be used to *refute* the perception you are challenging.
- It is also more *persuasive* to them.

Begin by referring back to the section *How do you uncover someone's perceptions?* Using the seven techniques there, write down as many of their perceptions as you can.

Go through your list and see which perception you could use to *refute* the belief you wish to challenge.

Then you've got to determine whether the new perception you have identified is more *persuasive* to them. So write down the two beliefs side by side, and think about which one is more important to them.

Consider the other person's values. Which belief do they hold more dear? Look at their record of behavior. In situations where the two beliefs have come into conflict, which one have they acted upon? You may wish to consult people who know and have observed the individual on many occasions.

Getting them to cooperate when they *refuse*

An overriding perception is so powerful, you can often use it to persuade someone to work with you on resolving the problem, even when initially they are determined not to.

Conventional wisdom says you can settle a dispute only if the other person is in a cooperative mood. But people who are fighting each other are rarely in a cooperative mood. It's *normal* for them to refuse to come together.

That doesn't mean the dispute is impossible to resolve. You can begin hashing out an issue without asking someone's permission—if you think strategically.

But take a look at what we typically do. Since we believe we can't negotiate without the other person's permission, we begin by asking, "Do you want to talk things out?"

Think twice before asking that.

By asking "Do you want to negotiate?" you may completely blow your chances of resolving anything.

Let's say you hire Dave the Contractor to remodel your kitchen, only to find that his bill is $750 beyond the price you agreed upon. When you inquire politely about this discrepancy, Dave the Contractor gets huffy and indignant.

At this point you are wondering if you will ever get Dave the Contractor to be reasonable unless you hire a hit man, which is one form of conflict resolution, so you ask Dave, "Can we discuss this?"

Sounds reasonable—but *not* strategic. Think about it: you are *already* discussing the bill; you don't need Dave's permission to continue. It's obvious he does not want to budge. So if you ask him to negotiate, what's he going to say?

You guessed it: *No!* He'll say there is nothing to negotiate!

If you want to work things out, it does not help to invite Dave to take a stand *against* working things out. That's what you end up doing by asking Dave, "Can we discuss this?"

Why will they refuse? Dave will say no because of his perceptions:

- "If I agree to negotiate, they'll think I'm ready to give in."
- "I could wind up giving endless concessions. Who knows how much I will have to give to satisfy them!"
- "I should not give a concession until I receive one."
- "There is no reason to negotiate now. I can always do it later if I want."
- "There's no point in reasoning with them. They're not open to changing their mind."
- "They are difficult to deal with. Why should I spend more time with them?"

Such perceptions often explain why someone refuses to negotiate. Note how logical they are. We think that someone who won't talk things out is irrationally hard-nosed. That's not the case here. Dave the Contractor is being rational. *He's responding to your invitation.*

Inviting someone to negotiate is like leading someone into a dark room and asking, "Do you like what you see?" It's like asking, "Will you buy this car?" without disclosing the price. You're asking the other person to make a commitment blindly, without much information. No wonder Dave says no.

We believe that if someone refuses to negotiate, there's no hope. That's not necessarily true. Often the problem is simply your approach.

Enticing them to negotiate. Here's an example of how the right approach can make the difference. A chemical company wished to build an incinerator to burn toxic waste. No problem, except that this was right next to a residential neighborhood. The neighborhood was comprised of discerning individuals who quickly concluded that fumes of toxic waste would not do wonders for their property values, not to mention their life expectancies.

The city council was split on whether to allow the incinerator to be built. Two council members were in favor, two were opposed, another was undecided. The mayor called me in to negotiate an agreement between the chemical company and the neighbors to address everyone's concerns.

The company's lawyer told me, "I'm eager to negotiate. Alas, [deep sigh of regret] the neighbors are not willing. You should ask them whether they're willing to compromise. I doubt they'll agree even to *meet.*"

Sound a little suspicious?

It sure did to me. I had a hunch the chemical company's lawyer *knew* the neighbors would refuse to get together. She *wanted* them to say no. She would delight in telling the council, "See, I told you! Those neighbors are so stubborn, even an expert mediator couldn't get them to the table. It's hopeless trying to work with them. Now there's no reason to delay building the incinerator."

She didn't want to compromise any more than the neighbors did. But she perceived that to win approval, her company had to *appear* open and responsive. Although she saw negotiation as bad, she had an overriding perception: "To win approval, I must appear reasonable." How could I harness that overriding perception, to entice her to negotiate?

I came up with this strategy: I told the neighbors, "To block the incinerator, you need to win over one undecided council member. He needs to see you're reasonable. How about inviting the company's lawyer to negotiate anywhere, anytime, no preconditions?" The neighbors gladly complied.

Take a wild guess who was furious.

You're right: the lawyer for the chemical company.

I'd called her bluff. No longer could she profess to be open to negotiation, and yet not negotiate. No longer could she have it both ways. She agreed to get together with the neighbors.

Initially, the neighbors were also opposed to negotiating, as well. Both sides chose to negotiate because they perceived that to win over a key council member, they had to appear reasonable.

I drew on their overriding perception that they had to *appear* reasonable, so that I could convince them in fact to *be* reasonable. *Use their own perceptions to convince them.*

What if they won't cooperate?

Conventional wisdom:	Strategic communication:
Invite the other person to meet and resolve things.	Beware of asking to negotiate! They may say no and dig in.
People are reasonable and will agree to talk things out.	People in a dispute often refuse to cooperate.
You can't settle an issue unless everyone is willing.	You can begin resolving things without asking permission.
If they refuse to negotiate, don't waste your time trying to get them to negotiate.	If they refuse to negotiate, use an overriding perception to entice them to negotiate.

If you dislike one perception of theirs, try another

There was a young man in New York who had just gotten his bachelor's degree. Like many college graduates, he had no idea what to do with it. He wondered, "What can I do with a BA in Biology?"

He thought of an idea. He went to Central Park and began taking people on what he called "eating tours" of the park. For seven dollars, he would show you all the things in the park that you could eat.

Well, the police found out about this and arrested him for destruction of park property.

A TV reporter got a tip that this man was sitting in jail. She burst in on a parks commissioner with camera running, and thrust a microphone in his face: "Mr. Commissioner, at this moment your park is infested with pimps, prostitutes and drug dealers—the dregs of society. Why are you spending our tax dollars to arrest an entrepreneur making an honest living, on some petty charge like 'eating in the park'?"

The parks commissioner did not respond to the TV reporter immediately. He took a moment to think about her perception. Then he smiled into the camera, "You don't understand. This man isn't eating *in* the park. He's *eating the park!*"

The reporter was instantly disarmed. The reason becomes evident when you examine her perception. She believed, "Eating in the park is no crime." But she had an overriding perception: *"Destroying* the park *is* a crime."

The commissioner invoked this overriding perception. He reframed the man's activity from "eating in the park" to destroying the park. In so doing, he defused an adversarial situation.

If someone's immediate perception is not useful to you, find another one that is. Get in the habit of asking yourself, "What are they thinking? What are their perceptions—and which ones should I build on?"

Don't get stuck focusing on a perception that's hard to deal with. Get creative and search for others.

THEN, BEFORE YOU MAKE YOUR APPROACH, double-check that it will actually work. At the very moment you seem so close to success, you certainly don't want to say something that makes the situation *worse*.

How can you assess whether your move will backfire?

That's where the final strategic step is key.

❖ *Key points for applying strategic step #3:* **Use their own perceptions to convince them**

1. Beware of thinking that "what they think is their problem." Their thinking is *your* problem, if you're trying to persuade them. People decide what to do based on their perceptions, not yours.
2. Use the seven techniques to uncover someone's perceptions:
    * Consider: From their perspective, why should they do what you want? Why shouldn't they?
    * Think about what they've said.
    * Look for patterns in their behavior.

- Ask them what they're thinking.
- Get advice from people who know them.
- Look behind one perception to find another.
- Brainstorm possible perceptions.

3. Make sure the other person sees that your request fits with their existing beliefs. Whenever someone hears a new idea, they compare it to their existing perceptions to see whether it makes sense. If your idea fits, they accept it. If not, they reject it.

4. Select which perception you will build on. If the other person is operating from a perception that is unfavorable to you, don't immediately get discouraged. Ask yourself what other perceptions they have.

5. Fight one of their perceptions with another. Arm yourself with an *overriding perception*, a belief of theirs that is more persuasive to them than the perception you wish to challenge.

6. Beware of asking to negotiate! They may say no and dig in. Instead, use an overriding perception to entice them to work with you on resolving things.

Predict the other person's response

You're all set to strike back, to "tell them a thing or two."
A word of advice.
DON'T.
Don't give them a piece of your mind.
USE *your mind.*
What you are about to say may make things worse. Often, such an outcome is predictable. This chapter shows you how to predict it.

Here's an experiment that you can try with your friends, perhaps at a party. I do it during conference presentations. I open up my wallet, take out a $20 bill, hold it up to the audience, and announce: "I am going to auction off this $20 bill. You are free to participate or watch. The choice is yours. But this is real. I am going to give this $20 bill to someone in this room, and I intend to collect.

"Now the ground rules: You can't make any side deals with anyone else in the room. The bidding will be in whole dollars, not cents. And there is one feature that will distinguish this auction from others: in addition to collecting from the highest bidder, I will also collect from the second-highest bidder. So if the two highest bids were $4 from Nancy and $3 from Bob, they would each pay me their bids, and Nancy would get the $20 bill.

"Now, who will offer me $1 for this $20 bill?"

The results are predictable. Someone yells out, "$3!" Another person calls out, "$4!" And other people make other offers until the bidding reaches about $13. Then bidders begin dropping out. Finally, only the two highest bidders are left.

That's when they suddenly feel the trap. If they refuse to bid higher, they risk being number two and losing everything. If they keep bidding, they may be number one but they will have to pay more for this $20 bill. Typically, each bidder would prefer to pay a little more, rather than lose everything. And so they keep topping each other.

How high do you suppose the bidding goes?

$17? $18? Would you be surprised to hear that the bidding almost always goes above $20?

It does.

Everyone roars with laughter when people bid $21, then $22, then $23, and more for a $20 bill. No matter how high the bidding goes, the logic is the same: wouldn't you prefer to bid a little more, rather than lose everything? And so the bidders keep bidding. Often up to $35. Sometimes higher.

How much would you guess the final bids were in my most successful auction? It was with a group of foreign executives at the University of California, Berkeley. The bidding had gone on for half an hour, and neither high bidder seemed ready to give in—even though they were each shaking with nervous tension. So to bring the auction to a close, I told them to write down their final bids. I told them to bid only as much as they could afford to lose.

One man, from Egypt, bid...$7,500. He lost.

The other man, from Latin America, bid...$15,000.

I have saved their bid slips to remind myself that this actually happened. (In case you're wondering, I did not collect on these bids. Normally, I collect checks made out to the winner's favorite charity, but alas, not this time.)

The $20 bill auction demonstrates a number of key points. First, when you take action, it's easy to overlook how the other person will respond. You enter the bidding because you're tempted by the lure of easy money. You want a $20 bill for $3 or $4. Sounds like a good deal.

You don't stop to consider how someone else is going to respond to your move. You don't stop to consider that if you submit a low bid, another bidder will be tempted to bid higher—and that then you will have to choose between forfeiting your bid and offering more.

If you do stop to consider the other person's response before you submit a bid, it's very easy to foresee the consequences. That's another point that the auction demonstrates: *human behavior is predictable.* So if you pause to predict someone's response, you can avoid such a foreseeable trap.

Human beings are predictable?

Yes, they are.

Human behavior *is* predictable

There is a popular notion that human beings are so complex that they defy prediction. In the previous chapter, I myself mentioned that people are not as predictable as chess pieces. I pointed out that it can be impossible to predict someone's actions four or five moves ahead.

But many of us have leaped to the conclusion that people are not predictable at all. And that's flat wrong.

Psychologists have demonstrated again and again:

human behavior *is* predictable. The whole discipline of experimental psychology is based on that fact. One of the ways that psychologists test a theory of human behavior is by seeing whether they can use it to predict what someone will do.

Take, for example, the theory that our perceptions shape our behavior. Remember how the UCLA researcher tested that theory? By using it to predict children's behavior. She went into an elementary school and gave kids a puzzle to work on. As you'll recall, she gave them so little time to do it that they all failed. But initially, she did not reveal that the task was impossible. Rather, she led one group of kids to believe that they failed because they lacked ability. She led another group to believe that they failed because they didn't try hard enough.

Then she gave all the kids another puzzle. Based on the theory that our perceptions shape our behavior, she *predicted* that the kids who believed they lacked ability would give up sooner on the new puzzle. She *predicted* that the kids who believed they didn't try hard enough would persist longer on the new task.

Sure enough, her predictions were right.

So don't be seduced by the myth that it is impossible to predict human behavior. As with any sort of prediction, a prediction of human behavior is not going to be right 100% of the time. Predicting someone's response is a bit like predicting the weather: you can't expect you'll always be right, but a good prediction will help you sidestep major trouble.

Should you anticipate someone's response?

Conventional wisdom:	Strategic communication:
You can't resolve a problem by predicting it.	You can prevent a problem by predicting it.
In fact, human behavior is unpredictable.	In fact, many common problems are predictable.
So don't bother trying to predict the future.	So consider what the other person is likely to do.

Your actions may be part of the problem

How many times have you walked away from an argument wondering: "How did that happen? How did things spiral out of control?" You can't understand how an insignificant quarrel escalated, maybe to the loss of a job or the breakup of a relationship. Since we never intend to arrive at such a negative outcome, we're always surprised when we do.

Yet, a lot of these negative outcomes—like the predicament in the $20 bill auction—are entirely predictable. It is possible to foresee them, and thus to avoid them. I'll give you an example. It involves a union spokesperson named Charlie. Management had just finished presenting its contract proposal. Charlie blurted out: "Is this the most you're willing to offer?"

The company negotiator snapped shut her briefcase and smiled, "Charlie, I'm glad you asked me that. We are not holding anything back. This is our final offer."

The color drained from Charlie's face as he realized what he had done. Unwittingly, he had invited his opponent to take a firm position *against him.* He had asked her to make a commitment—*when he didn't want her to get committed!*

He didn't want her to dig in.

So he shouldn't have *asked.*

Her response was entirely predictable. If before he spoke Charlie had paused to consider how she would respond, he could have avoided creating a problem for himself. Like Charlie, a lot of us fail to see, until it's too late, how we create problems for ourselves.

We see ourselves as innocently responding to the other person. We don't realize how our response, in turn, triggers a counter-reaction from them. In reality, everything you say is both a response to the other person and a stimulus for what they do next.

There is a cycle of action and reaction.

1. *I make a demand, you make a demand.*
2. *I explain my position, you explain yours.*
3. *I announce I'm digging in, you do the same.*
4. *I stop talking, you stop talking.*

That's the Talking Trap (discussed on page 50). When we're caught in this cycle, I may conclude—*you're* not cooperating!

But you *are* cooperating. You're continuing the cycle with me. You're responding—predictably—to my actions at each step.

We're reacting to each other. That's the hidden way we get sucked into a cycle of argument and escalation.

How we get emotionally hooked

When someone says something that piques your anger, what do you instinctively feel like doing? Striking back. You don't feel like considering how they will respond. You feel like striking back. It's a reflexive response.

When you get a check-up, and the doctor taps below your knee with a rubber mallet, what does your leg do? It kicks out reflexively. That's how you behave when you get emotionally hooked in a discussion. You respond reflexively.

Our reflexes ensnare us in arguments.

You see kids get ensnared all the time. Johnny, age 5, and Suzy, age 7, are slugging each other. You break up the fight and ask Johnny, "Why did you hit Suzy?" Johnny blurts: "Because Suzy hit me!"

Not exactly a model of strategic thinking. Johnny is not considering what he wants from Suzy, nor whether hitting her is the best way to get it.

There is zero thinking. It is all reflex.

A lot of disputes between adults are like this. You find yourself striking back automatically. Suddenly you're not thinking; you've lost sight of your purpose. You've lost control. Who *is* in control? Perhaps the other person, perhaps no one.

Slow down the conversation

When you're in the throes of an argument, you must maintain your focus on solving the problem. If the pace of give-and-take is too fast for you to think straight, don't try to keep up. Slow it down. When the other person says something, don't say something right back.

Pause. And in that pause, do two things. The first is by far the hardest:

1. *Don't say anything.*
2. Ask yourself, "If I say what I'm planning to say, how will the other person respond?"

When you're all set to strike back, to "set the record straight," to "make a few points," *pause.*

You may feel compelled to speak right away. You may find that you're uncomfortable with silence.

Get comfortable. Only if you take time to think during a conversation can you tell whether the words you are planning to say will actually help resolve the problem.

Often, they will make it worse. In addition to the Talking Trap, there are many other patterns in which you say something, the other side replies, suddenly there's a stalemate, and nobody knows what went wrong. I call these counterproductive patterns *dances to deadlock*, and they all have one thing in common.

They are predictable. If you pause to consider the other person's response, you can avoid these conversational routines. I'm going to tell you about three dances to deadlock: the Waltz to War, the Game of Endless Giving, and Tit-for-Tat.

The Waltz to War

The lawyer for the chemical company began doing this dance to deadlock intentionally. (You remember, she wanted the city to allow her to build an incinerator next to homes.) Recall her strategy: she wanted me to ask the neighbors whether they would budge; then they would refuse; then she could attack them as stubborn in front of the city council.

She was following the three steps of the Waltz to War:

1. *You ask your opponents: "Will you give in?"*
2. *Regrettably, they refuse.*
3. *You claim they are stubborn—and attack!*

The Waltz to War is a conversational routine where, intentionally or not, you entice the other person to take an opposing stand—which gives you the perfect excuse for attacking them.

Charlie the union man began the Waltz to War without knowing it. When he asked the company negotiator, "Is this the most you're willing to offer?" he was essentially asking, "Will you give in?" And when she, predictably, said no; he, unfortunately, laid into her: "But that's not reasonable! You can't just dig in like that! That's no way to have a discussion!"

Think about it: when you're in a conflict, do *you* like to give in? Of course not. You see, if someone asked you to give in, you'd naturally say no, too. You are a potential victim of the Waltz to War.

So what can you do if someone asks you whether you will compromise? The company negotiator felt she had to choose between backing down and digging in.

But there is another option. You can reinforce your position without locking yourself in. The company representative could have said, "This is the limit of my authorization." That would have left open the possibility that management might *change* her authorization.

The Game of Endless Giving

An excellent example of another dance to deadlock involves, as you might expect, alimony. A student of mine, Joy, approached me after class one night and said, "In my house, I'm the breadwinner. My husband sits on the sofa all day, watching TV, waiting for the employment agency to call. I'm getting a divorce. But I'm having trouble getting him to agree about how much alimony I'm going to pay him."

She began by offering him $300 a month. Her husband balked, "What?! You can afford more than that!"

She hesitated, "Well, I suppose if I get the promotion, as I expect, I could manage $350."

Her husband snapped, "You have got to be joking. Absolutely unacceptable."

She asked, "Well, how much *is* acceptable to you?"

He replied, "I'm sure we can work things out without lawyers. But you'll have to get realistic."

She reflected, "OK...well, let's make it $400. That's

the most I can do, without taking out a second mortgage on the house."

He still said no.

Joy told me, "This is impossible. No matter how much I give, he won't say yes."

I said: "Well, look at his perceptions. Why should he say yes? You keep giving more."

Joy was playing the Game of Endless Giving:

1. *You give concessions with nothing in return.*
2. *Those on the other side take your concessions.*
    Then they decide whether you've given enough.
    No surprise, they ask for more.
3. *You give more, to try to appease them.*
4. *They demand more, because for them this game is working well.*

When you're the victim in the Game of Endless Giving, you reward the other side for fighting you. They gain by rejecting your offers and demanding more. *And the longer they fight you, the more they can get.*

Giving more only makes things worse.   What's amazing is that when people find themselves caught in this pattern in which the more they give, the more they lose, their typical response is to give more!

Really. I collect newspaper articles with examples. A developer, Pete Grant, bought hundreds of acres along the coast north of San Francisco. He guaranteed that he would preserve 96% of the land as open space.

Did environmentalists applaud Pete Grant?

On the contrary. They sued him to stop him from building a resort on the remaining 4%.

Pete Grant felt betrayed. It's not hard to see why. Imagine his perceptions: "One concession deserves another. If I'm nice enough to preserve 96%, surely the environmentalists won't sue me to block my plans for a measly 4%."

This deal might have worked, but for one oversight. Mr. Grant neglected to get the environmentalists to *agree* not to sue. That was his big mistake. They might have accepted development *for something in return.* But now that he had already given them 96%, why shouldn't they push to preserve 100%?

Doubtless, that was *their* perception. Consequently, the environmentalists were willing to budge less after his concession than they had been before. Mr. Grant's concession caused their immediate limit to shrink. (Remember, their immediate limit is the most they're willing and able to do right now. The environmentalists were willing to do less after his concession.)

Mr. Grant's sense of betrayal is a hallmark of the Game of Endless Giving. You make a concession, and not only does the other side fail to reciprocate, they respond to your generosity with obstinacy!

Joy, the wife negotiating alimony, told me, "I may have a deadlock, but at least I have the satisfaction of knowing I tried. I offered all the money I had."

I don't know about you, but offering all my money is not the way I gain satisfaction.

Joy's dilemma could not be solved by giving money. (In a few pages, I'll tell you what she did.) When you're playing the Game of Endless Giving, giving concessions does not avert deadlock.

It *produces* deadlock.

But the answer is not to become intransigent. That can produce deadlock, too. So what is the moral?

Make sure you receive when you give. It may be better to give than to receive, but you'd better receive when you give, or you may not receive at all.

Pete Grant gave without receiving, and what happened to his development? It was tied up in court for years. Meantime, he went bankrupt. Ultimately, the environmentalists won—and the coast, literally, is clear.

Beware the Game of Endless Giving

Conventional wisdom:	Strategic communication:
You must give a concession to satisfy their demand.	The more you give, the *more* they may demand.
Keep giving concessions until they say yes.	If you keep giving more, they may never say yes.
You won't reach agreement unless you concede.	You may not reach agreement *if* you concede.

Tit-for-Tat

As an antidote to the Game of Endless Giving, some negotiation gurus suggest you play another game—Tit-for-Tat. The rule here is: you treat the other person the way that they treat you. If they are nice to you, you are nice to them. If they play hardball, you play hardball.

Playing Tit-for-Tat protects you from giving without receiving. And the idea of reciprocity seems fair. It sounds like the Golden Rule: "Do unto others as you would have others do unto you." Except that Tit-for-Tat says, "Do unto others as they *actually* do unto you."

This is not always a good idea.

Tit-for-Tat can make things worse. Let me tell you what happened when I called my local newspaper about a classified ad I had placed. I wanted to find out how long the ad was supposed to keep running.

The clerk barked, "What's your phone number?" This woman was *grumpy*. I gave her my phone number. No luck. Not listed in her computer.

I suggested, "I might have listed the ad under my work number." The clerk tried that. Again, no listing. I asked her to check under my last name.

"Nothing under that," she repeated.

She was sounding really irritated now. "It was a classified ad?"

"Yes."

She said condescendingly, "Well, you can't expect us to find your ad unless you give us the phone number." As if I should have known better than to call her.

"I understand." I apologized, "I'm sorry I'm giving you extra work. It's all my fault, for being so disorganized..."

She explained, "It's just kind of hard to find it, you know, unless we know the correct phone number." Her voice seemed to be softening.

I said, "Yes, I understand. I really appreciate your taking the time to check for me. I'm sorry this is turning out to be a nuisance. I didn't mean to cause you trouble."

Then she brightened, "Tell me this, do you know when the ad began running?"

I thought for a moment. "Gee...I'm not sure. I lost the paperwork. Probably last Sunday."

She said, "Because I was going to go look in last Sunday's paper. If that's the first day the ad appeared, the closing date will be printed in it."

This offer was clearly beyond the call of duty. I said, "Oh, that's very kind of you."

She said, "Well, I'll look and see." And she found the ad for me.

How did I entice this clerk to want to help me? How did I get her attitude to turn around?

You might think I used Tit-for-Tat. She was nice to me, so I was nice to her. But if you look carefully, you'll see that I was nice to her *before* she was nice to me. I was not playing Tit-for-Tat.

If I had been, imagine how the conversation would have gone. She had said condescendingly, "Well, you can't expect us to find your ad unless you give us the phone number." Playing Tit-for-Tit, I would have matched her tone and retorted, "I see I'll have to call back when there's a *competent* person available!" And if she had continued Tit-for-Tat and replied in kind, the conversation would have deteriorated fast.

Just as one good turn deserves another, so does one bad turn. That's a big problem with Tit-for-Tat. Reciprocity builds not only goodwill but also ill will.

Tit-for-Tat ignores your aim of resolving things. Whatever is happening in the conversation, whether it's constructive or destructive, Tit-for-Tat can magnify it. Tit-for-Tat performs this function whether or not it is helpful. Tit-for-Tat ignores the four strategic elements:

- *The problem.* Tit-for-Tat makes no allowances for a misunderstanding. Suppose this clerk had not meant to be rude. If I had snapped back at her, I would have fostered a negative cycle needlessly.
- *The goal.* What purpose would I have accomplished by lashing back at the clerk? What would I have gotten her to do? Absolutely nothing. In fact, she would have been *less* likely to help me after I insulted her.
- *The method.* What were this clerk's perceptions? Tit-for-Tat says: Who cares? Ignore what they're thinking. Simply respond in kind.
- *The result.* If you mirror their actions, what will they do in return? Tit-for-Tat says: Damn the consequences; reciprocate their behavior anyway.

Of course, if they're doing the same mindless dance, and they're as stubborn as you are, escalation is inevitable. Then you find yourself in intellectually stimulating conversations like:

"You're being unreasonable!"

"I'm not being unreasonable, you are!"

"Oh, yeah?"

"Yeah!"

This is the frequent outcome of Tit-for-Tat—both sides badgering, pestering, prodding, pressuring, urging, nagging, and above all, repeating themselves— mirror images of each other.

How can you escape a dance to deadlock?

The first step to getting out of a negative pattern is recognizing that you're caught in it. That's difficult because you rarely make an informed choice to do a dance to deadlock. Rather, you become ensnared.

In the Waltz to War, you never choose to go to war. The other person asks, "Will you give in?" You respond honestly, saying no—and suddenly, you're trapped. The other person has set you up and now has an excuse to attack.

In the Game of Endless Giving, you're rarely aware that you are giving more and more concessions, nor that you are encouraging them to dig in and hold out. As far as you know, you are simply trying to satisfy them.

And in Tit-for-Tat, you don't realize that mirroring the other person's behavior could be harmful to your own interests. You're doing this dance because it seems fair ("I'll treat them as they treat me").

All of these dances are seductive. You may feel stupid for doing them, but you aren't. Reasonable people engage in self-defeating behavior for reasonable reasons—but without seeing what they're really doing. So how can you tell if you're caught in a negative cycle?

Monitor the conversation as it's happening. Are you accomplishing anything? Is talking helping? One warning sign is when you hear yourself saying the same thing over and over without results. Other red flags include: name-calling, sniping, bullying, sudden deafness, denial, rejection, stubbornness, and rigid declarations.

Monitor your emotions. Get in the habit of checking how you're feeling during the conversation. Do you feel yourself getting angry? Frustrated? Digging in? Is your stomach tightening? Your heart pounding faster? Your breathing quickening? Those are all signs that your emotions may have taken over and that you may be hooked.

What can you do then?

Call time out. "Let me think about it and get back to you." Or: Secretly make your beeper go off. Put your finger on your nose and say you've got a nosebleed. You have to go to the bathroom. The kids are waiting for you at day care. Anything. Just get out of there.

Step away and regain your composure, so you can think straight.

Recognize the dance you're doing. I've pointed out common dances to help you recognize them. Think back to your conversation: What did each person say? How did the other react? Then refer to the descriptions of negative patterns in this chapter to help you identify the dance you're doing.

Once you see the pattern, you gain the power to change your behavior to avert the consequences.

Break the cycle. How can you possibly break the cycle? Simple. When the person tries to continue the dance, *don't cooperate.* For example, in the Game of Endless Giving, when they say, "You've got to do better than that," don't give yet another concession. Do something different, to break the action-response pattern. (To develop your next move, review the four strategic steps: *decide whether you have a misunderstanding or a true disagreement, create the other person's next move, use their own perceptions to convince them,* and *predict the other person's response.*)

I'll tell you how Joy applied this advice when her husband kept pushing for more alimony. She identified his perceptions; he was thinking, "As long as she's giving, I might as well keep pushing." How did she use this perception to convince him to settle?

She stopped giving. She stood up to him. She said, "I've made a lot of concessions. Now I'd like to see some movement from you."

He pressed, "I think $450 a month would be a more reasonable range."

She countered, "If I get the BMW and a few other things, I might be willing to consider $400."

Now Joy was no longer doing her husband's dance. Quite the opposite. She was demanding a concession from *him*. This caught him off guard: *"You're* asking for the BMW? *I* want the BMW."

She replied, "Well, *I* want to pay less than $400."

He pushed a few more times, but when he saw she was holding firm, he gave up.

She broke the cycle. The moral is: When you recognize a negative pattern, *stop responding according to the pattern.*

Unfortunately, human nature is to continue the cycle. How do you get into the Talking Trap? By explaining your point of view. That's exactly your inclination about how to get out of it.

This instinct makes as much sense as eating garlic to cure garlic breath. More of the same only makes things worse.

Avoiding traps in predicting behavior

When you develop a plan, and you're excited about the prospect of success, there is a tendency to focus on how you *want* the other person to respond, and to ignore what they're *likely* to do.

This is a common pitfall in predicting behavior. And one of my clients, the president of an American computer company, fell right into it.

His company operated by the motto, "Ship it now; if it breaks, we'll fix it later." He was so obsessed with meeting shipping deadlines, his company didn't adequately test the computers before the products left the factory.

It wasn't long before the computers began breaking

down at customer sites around the world. The company didn't have enough technicians to repair them all.

So, the company's largest customer, a Japanese firm, offered to send their own technicians to America to study the blueprints and learn how to fix the computers on their own.

I advised my client: "This is not a bright idea. They will learn how to *manufacture* the computers."

He replied, "No, no, no. They don't want to get into the manufacturing business! They just need to *understand* how we make computers so they can repair them. Then they'll be satisfied."

Classic case of the Great Myth of Hidden Harmony ("Deep down, we all agree"). He assumed that the goals of the two companies were in synch.

Six months later, this corporate president had to lay off a third of his employees. The Japanese had gone into business manufacturing the computers themselves.

How could he have been so blind to this possibility?

Because he *wanted* to believe there would be no problem. He was an optimist, but not a realist.

Just as a typical error in predicting behavior is to assume the best, the opposite tendency is also common: you're so upset at the other person that you assume they'll do the worst.

Four questions to predict their response. To steer you clear of both pitfalls, there are four simple questions you can ask yourself. These four questions help you differentiate what you want, what you fear, and what you're likely to get.

By prompting you to consider each factor separately, the four questions can help you predict someone's response with greater accuracy:

1. *From your perspective, what is the BEST response the other person could make?*
2. *What's the WORST response they might make?*
3. *What response do you EXPECT from the other person, based on their perspective?*
4. *Is the potential gain of your approach WORTH the risk?*

Applying the four questions

When Naomi and I were planning our wedding, the biggest headache was finding a location. Naomi had spent weeks on the phone and leafing through brochures. Then one night over dinner with my folks, she announced, "I finally found the place for the wedding!"

We started discussing the details and my father asked, "How many people can this place hold?"

Naomi responded, "120 guests, as we'd discussed." (This was already more people than she wanted.)

My father hesitated, "But we expanded the guest list to include my friends from work, remember?"

Naomi glanced up from her plate and said, "I wasn't aware of that. How many people are we talking about?"

My father replied, "About twenty."

Naomi looked alarmed. "Twenty?!"

I quickly intervened and suggested we hold a separate party for my dad's friends. My father looked pained. "I'd really like to invite them to the wedding. I mean, I *have* worked with them for 25 years."

Naomi was getting agitated. She and my father had gotten along so well until tonight, I didn't want their relationship to become strained over this. But if they kept talking, given the frustration on both sides, I was afraid the discussion could escalate into an argument.

I dabbed my mouth with my napkin, pushed my chair back and smiled at everyone, "Where has the time gone? Well, we'd better get going!"

As we left, Naomi said, "David, I can't go through all this hassle. Would *you* please discuss this with your dad?"

Great. As I drove home that night with my betrothed, three approaches immediately came to mind for dealing with my father:

A. Ask him, for the sake of family harmony, not to invite his twenty friends.

B. Invite Dad to sit down with Naomi to develop some mutually satisfactory solution.

C. Help Dad find a way to convince Naomi to accept his twenty friends.

Which approach would be best?

The best approach to take depends on how the other person will respond. So let's evaluate how Dad would respond to each approach.

Approach A: Ask Dad, for the sake of family harmony, not to invite his twenty friends.

1. *From my perspective, what's the BEST response Dad could make?*

   The best response would be, "Okay, I won't invite them."

2. *What's the WORST response Dad might make?*

   He might say, "You're asking me to disregard my friends because you're on *Naomi's* side!"

3. *What response do I EXPECT from Dad, based on his perspective?*

   He'd say, "I don't see why 'family harmony' requires me to ignore my friends. I've worked with these people for 25 years, and I'd like them to be at the wedding."

4. *Is the potential gain of my approach WORTH the risk?*

   No way. This approach probably wouldn't help, and it could make things worse.

Approach B: Invite Dad to meet with Naomi to brainstorm a mutually acceptable solution.

1. *From my perspective, what's the BEST response Dad could make?*

   He could agree to meet, and once he talked to Naomi, he might see things her way and compromise—perhaps suggesting that he invite ten friends from work instead of twenty.

2. *What's the WORST response Dad might make?*

   He might refuse to discuss it. Or he might meet

with Naomi, restate his position, and when she balked he might get annoyed.

3. *What response do I EXPECT from Dad, based on his perspective?*

He might meet with her as a favor to me, but he would still want to invite all his friends.

4. *Is the potential gain of my approach WORTH the risk?*

No. The potential gain would be minimal. And there would be a risk that if my father and Naomi met, they would only get more aggravated and frustrated.

Often, we assume that the solution to a problem is to urge people to meet and talk it out. We fail to think realistically about what we expect them to do when they meet. Deep down, we are hoping that when they hear each other's views, they will exclaim, "You're right! I never realized that before!" and they will be willing to compromise.

But Naomi and my father already understood each other. They had a true disagreement.

Approach C: Help Dad find a way to convince Naomi to accept his twenty friends.

1. *From my perspective, what's the BEST response Dad could make?*

The best response would be, "Okay, let's try to get her to say yes."

2. *What's the WORST response Dad might make?*

He might say, "Look, I don't want to deal with this issue. She's your fiancée, you deal with it."

3. *What response do I EXPECT from Dad, based on his perspective?*

He wanted to get Naomi to accept his friends. He'd either welcome my suggestions or he'd ask me to try to persuade her.

4. *Is the potential gain of my approach WORTH the risk?*

Certainly yes. Even if he asked me to play mediator, the situation then would be no worse than it was now.

What I did in real life. I used the four questions to anticipate Dad's response and spot the potential problems with each approach. Then I took approach C.

I said to him, "Let's focus on Naomi's immediate limit—how much she's willing to do right now. Is she willing to accept your twenty friends now?"

Dad sighed, "I don't think so."

"Why not?"

He said, "Because of all the extra work. She's finally found a place for 120 guests, and now she has to figure out how to accommodate twenty more."

I concluded, "So you're really asking her to do two things: accept more people and do more work. What if you broke the problem apart and asked her to take a smaller step. What if you asked her to accept more people if *you* did the extra work."

Dad nodded. "Sure, I could do that. I could talk to the manager at the location she's found. If necessary, I could check out other sites that meet her criteria."

Dad's overture won Naomi over. If he worked out

the logistics, she would go along with inviting his twenty co-workers.

However, the "right answer" in this case really is not that important. The right approach to take will depend on the situation.

What's important is *how* we identified the right approach, the thinking process I've been demonstrating. Remember these four questions to predict someone's response. They can help you spot flaws in your plan so you can modify it. They can also alert you when you need more information—perhaps about the worst way the person might respond or about what they're likely to do.

We need to retrain ourselves

Ask people from England. Or India. Or Nigeria. Or Canada. They'll tell you that Americans are known for "shooting first and asking questions later." For "charging in with guns blazing."

We are not known throughout the world for pausing to consider. Not Americans. We Americans are known for yelling, "Damn the torpedoes! Full speed ahead!" That battle cry is as old as the Civil War. We still say it, because we still believe it. In the movies, our heroes are people like John Wayne. The Lone Ranger. Dirty Harry. Rambo.

These are not deep thinkers. These are not people who think much at all. These are "men of action." They are not careful. They are reckless. They disregard what will happen. They do what they want to do

anyway. That is how our heroes on the screen behave. And we emulate them!

No surprise, then, that as adults we find ourselves charging into situations and blurting out things...that we instantly regret. We don't stop to assess the consequence of what we say before we say it. We find ourselves doing that assessment *afterwards*, when we realize, "Gee, did I blow it!"

Our cultural conditioning is 180 degrees away from strategic communication. *We've got to retrain ourselves.* We've got to train ourselves to remind ourselves throughout the conversation: "If I say what I'm planning to say, how will the other person respond?" With an estimate of how they'll respond, you can either prepare for their response or change your approach to avoid it. Either way, you're further ahead.

❖ *Key points for applying strategic step #4:* **Predict the other person's response**

1. Reflect on how you yourself are contributing to the problem. Often, we see ourselves as innocently responding to the other person. We don't realize how our response, in turn, triggers a counter-reaction from them. If you can identify what you're doing wrong, you gain the power to change it.

2. If the pace of give-and-take is too fast for you to think straight, don't try to keep up. Slow it down. Pause before replying to the other person. And ask

yourself, "If I say what I'm planning to say, how will they respond?"

3. To avoid getting emotionally hooked in a discussion:
    - *Monitor the conversation* as it's happening. Observe whether you're caught in a negative cycle and whether you're accomplishing anything.
    - *Monitor your emotions,* too, to see whether you're losing your cool.

4. If you're already caught in a dance to deadlock:
    - Call time out.
    - Recognize the dance you're doing. (Refer to the dances in this chapter, such as the Talking Trap, the Waltz to War, the Game of Endless Giving, and Tit-for-Tat.)
    - Break the cycle.

5. Use the four questions to predict their response:
    - From your perspective, what is the BEST response the other person could make?
    - What's the WORST response they might make?
    - What response do you EXPECT from the other person, based on their perspective?
    - Is the potential gain of your approach WORTH the risk?

THE STRATEGIC STEPS IN ACTION

Strategic questions and answers

Should you stand firm?
Should you make the
first offer? Should you
reveal information?
And why can't we
skip all the games?
As you start
using strategic
communication,
you're bound to have
questions. This chapter
provides answers.

W hen the other person refuses to budge, you may get so frustrated that you feel like punishing or harassing them until they give in. Or, at the other extreme, you may prefer to use the "win-win" strategy of continuing to cooperate, hoping that they will reciprocate.

Both approaches are habitual ways of dealing with differences. They often feel comfortable because they are familiar—even though they may be inappropriate to the present situation.

When you're under pressure and wondering what to do, the familiar ways of dealing with people come instantly to mind. One of the most common pitfalls in applying strategic communication is backsliding—sliding back into your old habits of thinking and behaving.

The approaches of punishing and cooperating may appear to be diametrically opposed philosophies. But they do have one thing in common.

They both can make things worse.

The strategy of making them suffer

There's a myth that when someone is obstinate, the one sure-fire way to get them to change is to inflict pain. Like the captain of the chain gang in *Cool Hand Luke*, you harass, embarrass, pressure, penalize, or threaten the other person until they give in. You teach them a lesson. They'll never mess with *you* again.

In reality, inflicting pain often fails to persuade the other person, because of their perceptions:

- "This punishment is no worse than I had expected." When the other person decided to oppose you, they anticipated you'd inflict some pain. They chose to endure it. If the pain you impose is no worse than what they had feared, you give them no reason to change their mind.
- "I can live with it." Even if the other person had not foreseen how bad your punishment would be, they learn to adapt to it. They may prefer to do that than to yield to pressure.
- "I'm so committed to my beliefs, I won't surrender no matter what." People refuse on principle to back down to bullying. Their principles are worth the pain.
- "I will not be humiliated." To surrender to pressure is to lose face. They'd be publicly admitting either that they were wrong or that they are weak.
- "I would set a precedent by caving in to pressure." They'd be telling you that whenever you want something from them, all you have to do is to make them suffer. This might encourage you to increase the pain to get even more.
- "I'm going to teach *you* a lesson." Even as you're trying to teach them a lesson, they're trying to teach you one: "You can't mess with me. I'm tough. *I* won't back down. So *you'd* better back down."

People can resist the worst punishment. If you have any doubt, you don't need to watch a work of fiction like *Cool Hand Luke*. Look at how the Japanese responded to US bombing during World War II. US General Marshall reported: "The Japanese had demonstrated in each case they would not surrender and they fight to the death. . .We had had 100,000 people killed in Tokyo in one night of bombs and it had seemingly no effect whatsoever." Japanese morale seemed as strong as ever.

"So," the general concluded, "It seemed quite necessary, if we could, to shock them into action."

That was the rationale for dropping the atomic bomb. It was dropped on Hiroshima, and 80,000 people were killed instantly. Birds ignited in midair. Some people burned to cinders while standing up. Others tried to ease their pain by plunging shrieking into rivers. After such extreme suffering, you might have thought the Japanese would have surrendered instantly. Yet, three days later, there was no plea for mercy. No sign of surrender. Nothing from Japan at all.

That's why, on the fourth day after dropping the atomic bomb on Hiroshima, the US decided to drop a second atomic bomb on Nagasaki. 70,000 people died there. Still Japanese leaders were divided on pursuing the war. The War Minister wanted to keep fighting. He preferred to die with honor than to surrender.

People are so strong-willed that even the threat of obliteration may not get them to change their minds.

Consider: Is applying pressure a good way to get *you* to change your mind? I've asked that question in a room of 500 people, and nobody raises a hand. Now suppose you're up against someone who's more stubborn than you are. If *you* won't back down to coercion, how can you expect *them* to?

A combative approach can easily backfire. I saw a woman cussing out a porter at the airport. I walked up to him afterwards and remarked, "You took a lot of abuse." The porter winked at me, "That's all right. That woman is going to Dallas. I've made sure her luggage is going to Seattle."

When you bully someone, they may get back at you in ways you don't suspect. You also risk damaging the relationship.

When you're frustrated, you may think of harassment or punishment as a sure-fire answer. But the approach of making them suffer, whether through the severest pain or the mildest harassment, may not be effective for resolving your particular problem.

When *does* harassment or punishment work? To answer that question, let's take a look at a few cases when it has been used both effectively and ethically.

Parents harass their kids to get them to do homework.

The bank threatens to penalize you unless you pay your mortgage on time.

Ethical harassment even helped a little Jewish boy escape Communist Poland. He was growing up there facing fierce discrimination. For years his parents had been longing for him to escape and have a better life in

America where his uncle lived. It was almost impossible to get official approval to leave.

Then one day, his parents heard that friends of theirs, a family with twelve kids, had by some miracle managed to get permission. They asked the mother, "Could you sneak out a thirteenth child—our son?" She agreed.

The night they were due to leave, the mother told all thirteen kids that when they got to the border they should behave as they normally did, only more so: they should hit each other, scream, cry, and run all over the place.

Above all, she told them to *keep moving.*

She knew the Polish guard would figure: "There's a long line of people to process, and these kids are impossible. I'll never be able to round them up and make them stand still long enough to count them."

And she was right. The guard threw up his hands and let them all through.

She caused trouble for the guard, and he gave in to get rid of her. Whether you harass, pressure, threaten or punish the other person, the basic strategy is the same: you cause trouble for them, and they give in to get rid of you.

The mother succeeded because she drew upon the guard's perception that, practically speaking, counting all the kids would be impossible.

So: What determines whether harassment or punishment will persuade?

The other person's perceptions.

Why did the mom *succeed?* Because of the perception of the Polish guard. Why did the bombing of Tokyo *fail* to get the Japanese to surrender? Because of the Japanese perceptions. The success or failure of any approach depends on the other side's perceptions.

"Win-win" is no answer

Just as many of us believe in the strategy of making the other person suffer, a lot of us believe in the opposite approach—cooperation. The "win-win" philosophy is: you help them toward their goal, then they'll help you toward yours. When they win, you win.

It would be nice if real life always worked this way.

Your goals often clash. In reality, often you don't *want* to support their objective. In some cases, it would even be morally repugnant to do so.

Imagine the win-win philosophy applied to Adolph Hitler. It was, courtesy of Neville Chamberlain, British prime minister. Chamberlain said in effect, "Mr. Hitler, we'll acquiesce in your goal of taking part of Czechoslovakia, so long as you promise not to take the rest." Did this win-win agreement resolve England's conflict with Germany? Hardly. It intensified it. Hitler, emboldened, went on to take not only *all* of Czechoslovakia but also Poland, as well, ultimately leading to war with Great Britain. Chamberlain's agreement is perhaps modern history's most dramatic example refuting the win-win credo.

Consider a more everyday case: A police chief had a habit of making sexist comments in public, and he wanted to continue speaking his mind, uncensored. That was his goal. "Freedom of speech," he called it. The mayor, on the other hand, was an ardent feminist. She certainly did not want to cooperate toward his goal of unrestrained self-expression, yet that's exactly what she ended up doing—because she was so imbued with the win-win spirit.

She tried to resolve the problem by being nice and cooperative, and thus, like Neville Chamberlain, she abetted it.

Whenever the chief would say something so profoundly stupid that the newspaper would run a story about it, the mayor would pull him aside and whisper: "Pete, you've got to stop making these sexist comments. People are getting upset."

But the chief kept doing it. Why?

He honestly thought the mayor didn't care. His perceptions were: "She is telling me to stop because she has to, for her public image. If she really cared, she'd get tough with me."

Sure enough, when the mayor threatened to fire him, the chief's behavior suddenly changed. (Her threat was another ethical example of the strategy of making them suffer.)

Should you take a position?

"Win-win" advocates say there's no need to take a stand to settle an issue. They say a hard position is inherently counterproductive. When you run into trouble, you're supposed to keep cooperating.

That's a lousy rule of thumb. Neville Chamberlain proved it; so did the mayor dealing with the police chief.

She had warned him to stop, many times. Given his perceptions, he would not have stopped unless the mayor had taken a stand. Will the other person get mad when you get tough? Often, they will. But thank goodness the mayor stopped taking a cooperative, lenient attitude toward the chief.

Her "win-win" attitude had prolonged the problem.

Taking a firm position resolved it. She had to convey what she wanted him to do and what would happen if he failed to change.

Reconsider the "win-win" approach

"Win-win" wisdom:	Strategic communication:
When you win, they win.	When they win, you may lose.
Help them toward their goal, so they will help you.	Before helping them, decide whether you support their goal.
To get them to cooperate, you must cooperate with them.	Sometimes you must stand firm before they'll cooperate.

Of course, you should take a stand only when it is strategically appropriate. If you habitually walk in to the room and announce, "Here's my position, take it or leave it!" you risk making things worse.

But if you review the four strategic steps and determine that taking a stand is the best thing to do, for heaven's sake, don't let the win-win credo discourage you from doing what is strategically wise. (Again, the four strategic steps are: *decide whether you have a misunderstanding or a true disagreement, create the other person's next move, use their own perceptions to convince them,* and *predict the other person's response.*)

Why can't we skip all the games?

Is it really necessary to push back and forth?

Some people try to "cut out the games" by suggesting that everyone come right out and say what they're ultimately willing to accept—their bottom line. I was coaching a chief executive on negotiation strategy to settle a lawsuit. He told me, "I want to avoid haggling. Let's tell the other side we'll give them $2,000,000 and no more."

I warned, "I wouldn't suggest that.."

He insisted, "They'd be happy to get $2,000,000! They'd be happy to get $1,800,000!"

I said, "They will be happy only if they think they're squeezing the most out of you they can. Whatever offer you make, they will test. They'll push, and they'll expect you to move some; they'll push again, and you'll move a bit less; they'll push a third time and you'll move even less. Only then will they be satisfied they've gotten the most possible."

He said, "Well, I want to shortcut all that. I'm going to tell them my offer, and if they say no, I won't give them anything."

I said, "Then we'll reach a stalemate."

He said, "I don't believe it!"

Well, the two sides met, and the chief executive announced, "I'm tired of all this back-and-forth stuff! So I'm going to cut to the chase. I'm going to lay my cards on the table right here and now, and then we can all go home and spend this evening with our families. $2,000,000."

The other company's representative slowly took out his pen. He held it in front of his eyes.

He rotated it. He examined it.

And while this demonstration with the pen was taking place, you could see the face of my chief executive cloud over.

The other guy put his pen back in his pocket and said, "I'll have to digest your offer."

The chief executive jumped up and bellowed, *"Digest!"* I thought he was going to strangle the guy. He said, "There'll be no *digesting.* You'll say yes or I'll see you in court!"

No surprise, he saw them in court.

The other side wasn't ready to settle until they had a chance to do "game-playing."

Whenever the other side keeps pushing, and you get annoyed, as the chief executive did, and you think, "Why can't they accept my word that I can't give any more!" remember: *Testing by pushing is a natural part of the process of resolving problems.*

People test to decide whether to agree. One way people judge whether an agreement is worth signing is by asking themselves: "Could I reach a better agreement with this person?"

Even if you could prevent them from testing your position, in so doing you would be preventing them from resolving any nagging doubts about how much you're willing to give.

You don't want them to have second thoughts ("Gee...I wonder if I could have done better if only I had pushed harder"). You don't want them to feel cheated. You want them to feel satisfied. If *they* are satisfied, there is less trouble for *you*.

Often in an adversarial confrontation, it is impossible to avoid the testing process. And it serves very useful purposes:

- It relieves nagging doubts.
- It makes them more satisfied.
- It gives them a feeling of assurance that they are making a wise decision by saying yes.

Should you reveal information?

The chief executive showed his hand and lost big. Which reinforces a common notion that information is power and that to keep power you should withhold information.

This notion is simplistic.

My student Lois was looking for a job and got a phone call from a prospective boss. She told me: "He kept asking how interested I was and I said as little as possible. I figured, *Don't give out information*. Right?"

Wrong. Look at his perception. Lois' prospective

boss believed, "If she's interested in the job, she'll show enthusiasm." If she didn't, he might hire someone else. After thinking it over, Lois wrote him a note about how much she'd enjoy working at his firm.

A lot of us refuse to reveal anything in a negotiation because we're afraid of losing power. But withholding information does not inherently give you power. Making the right decision about what to reveal gives you power.

In other words, a sound *strategy* gives you power.

Lois made a sound strategic decision to convey enthusiasm. She also made a sound decision not to mention that she had been out of a job for nine months. She was not revealing all the information she had. She was deciding what to reveal and what to conceal based on how the other person would respond.

Before you reveal something, predict the person's response. Consider whether revealing the information will help you or hurt you. (Of course, there are times when ethically you've got to reveal information that harms your interests. Like when you accidentally dent a parked car and leave a note taking responsibility.)

Should you make the first offer? When it came time to discuss salary, Lois wondered whether to reveal her aspiration or to let her prospective boss make an offer first. I asked her, "Based on your resume, how much would he think he has to offer you?"

Lois answered, "Around $40,000."

I asked, "Could he afford that? Is that within his immediate limit?"

She replied, "Yes. I've got a friend at that company and she says that's at the top of his pay range."

I pressed, "So you couldn't get any more?"

She said, "Probably not."

I suggested: "Then let him proceed on the basis of his perception that he's got to offer you $40,000."

So, should you be the first to reveal your position? Here, the answer was no. Lois' prospective boss was at his immediate limit. He thought that he had to offer her the most he could—$40,000. There was nothing more she could gain now.

Hypothetically, suppose his immediate limit were still $40,000, but that he perceived she would accept less ($33,000). Now would she benefit by being the first to propose a salary figure?

Yes.

Now Lois could demand something toward the high end, say, $38,800. She knows he can afford to pay $40,000. If her demand is credible, he'll realize that his initial expectation of $33,000 is unrealistically low. He'll see that he has to pay her more.

By being the first to reveal your position, you can shape the other person's expectations.

Here's a rule of thumb about whether you should make the first offer: in general, you can benefit by making the first offer *if your offer violates their expectations and is still within their immediate limit.* In our hypothetical scenario, Lois' offer is $38,800—violating her boss' expectation ($33,000) and still within his immediate limit ($40,000).

Don't give out information...right?

Conventional wisdom says:	Strategic communication says:
Information is power.	Strategy gives you power.
Don't reveal your position.	*Think* about what to disclose.
Say as little as possible.	Say as much as will help.

How much should you ask for?

Why should Lois go in requesting only $38,800? If she wants as much as she can get, shouldn't she ask for $40,000? Or even $45,000?

Well, remember, if you're in Lois' position, the most you can expect to get is $40,000—the boss' immediate limit. But that may be different from the amount you should initially request. *The right amount to request in your opening offer depends on the other person's perceptions about negotiating.*

Consider two typical examples.

The bargainer's mindset. Suppose the prospective boss perceives that a first offer is a wish, a hope, never to be taken very seriously. He believes, "You always bargain down a first offer." If that's his perception, and you go in asking for exactly what you want, you probably won't get it. If you want $40,000, and you ask for $40,000, he'll say no, he'll try to bargain you down, and in the end you'll be lucky to get $35,000.

If the other person has a bargainer's mindset, the rule is: go in asking for more than their immediate limit will allow. You won't lose the deal by asking for more, because they won't take your first offer seriously, anyway.

If you want $40,000, you might ask the boss for $42,000 or even $45,000, depending on how much he thinks he should bargain you down.

This allows for "bargaining room"—room for the other side to dicker you down to the figure you really expect to get. If you allow for bargaining room and make an opening offer of $45,000, then when the haggling is over, presumably you'll get a salary around $40,000.

There are many cultures in which most people have a bargainer's mindset. Some Americans think that haggling is inherently deceitful, because one minute you are saying you want one figure and then the next minute you are admitting that you would really settle for less. But when everyone tacitly understands the rules of the game, by definition there is nothing deceitful about haggling.

If you are dealing with someone who has the bargainer's mindset, and you fail to recognize it and adapt your strategy, you risk getting taken.

The "honesty" mentality. Now let's say you're negotiating salary with a prospective boss who believes in "open, honest communication." He thinks that people should be open about what they really want. He shoots straight, and he believes that you should, too. If you name a figure, he believes that you're serious about it.

When it comes to negotiating salary, he thinks that

you should honestly say what you need, and if he can give it to you, he will. If he can't, he will say no and there will be no deal. He will make no counter offer. Why? Because he trusts that you are honest in telling him what you need. If you were to accept a counter offer for less money, that would imply that you were being less than honest in your original figure, that you overstated it to manipulate him.

Now remember, his immediate limit is $40,000.

If you go into his office demanding $42,000, take a moment to predict his response. If his perceptions about negotiating are as I have described, then he will say no and there will be no deal. He will say, "Sorry, I would have liked to have hired you, but I don't have that big a budget."

Suppose you reply, "Oh, well, I could accept $40,000."

Based on his "honesty" perspective, how will he respond? He'll say: "Well, if your bottom line was $40,000, why didn't you say so? Why weren't you playing straight with me?"

As far as he is concerned, your credibility is now history. And so is your job application.

If you're dealing with someone with the "honesty" mentality, the rule is: make sure your request is within their immediate limit.

So, if you know that the boss' immediate limit is $40,000, you should go in asking for $40,000...right?

Not so fast. Pause to predict his response.

Suppose he will respond to a request for $40,000 by

getting concerned: if he hires you at the top of his pay scale, he won't be able to give you a promotion to a higher salary; within a year or two, you may get disgruntled.

Or suppose he'll respond by thinking that you are being greedy by asking for the most he can afford.

If you anticipate that he will respond negatively to an initial request that is at his immediate limit of $40,000, you'd do better to back off and ask for something a little less...like $38,800.

Before you make any offer, predict the other person's response. To determine how much to request, learn the other person's perceptions about the bargaining process. (See *How do you uncover someone's perceptions?*, page 128.)

Be ready to seize the moment

Just because the boss is willing to offer $40,000 today does not mean he'd be willing to do so tomorrow. Remember, a person's immediate limit can change. If a strategic moment appears, and you dawdle, there is a risk that in the meantime the other person will change their mind and that you will lose everything.

That is what happened to Lois. She got a final offer of $40,000 and hemmed and hawed about accepting it. A few days later, the boss called her back to say the company was being reorganized and all hiring was being put on hold.

Lois assumed that the offer would always be there for her to accept. This is a common assumption; I'm guilty of it myself. When I was 11 years old, I would throw my dirty clothes on the floor of my room and walk on them. One day my mother came to me and said, "I'm tired of asking you to pick up your clothes. They wear out faster if you walk on them, the room stinks, and it bugs me. So from now on, I'm not doing your laundry unless you keep your clothes off the floor for a whole week." She figured if I wanted my laundry done, I would pick up my clothes.

Well, she was wrong. I wasn't going to let *her* change *me*. I'd show *her*. I kept throwing my clothes on the floor. Meantime, my mother taught me how to work the washer and dryer. She was very happy. She was free of my laundry! She had set up the situation so that no matter what I did, she'd win. Either I'd clean up my room, or she'd be free of my laundry.

One year later, I realized I'd been had.

I brought her to my room, opened the door, and pointed proudly: "Look, Mom, I've kept my clothes off the floor for a whole week!"

She said, "I'm sorry, David, I've gotten accustomed to being free of your laundry. I'm not interested in doing your laundry now." I was *furious*. I stomped, "That's not fair! You didn't say it was a limited-time offer!" She said, "I couldn't foresee that you'd wait a year. This is a life lesson. When an opportunity comes along, you've got to take it."

Be alert to an opportunity in disguise. As a kid, I naturally assumed that my mother's sole purpose in life was to do my laundry. I did not recognize that her threat to stop washing my clothes was actually an offer to continue washing them (if I cleaned up my floor).

An opportunity frequently does not appear to be an opportunity. Frequently, it does appear as a threat.

In an earlier chapter I told you about Bob's argument with his landlord about breaking his lease. The landlord thinks Bob must pay a fee for moving out early; Bob disagrees.

The landlord says, "If you're refusing to pay, I will refer the matter to our attorneys. Perhaps you'd like to speak to them."

She means this as a threat, but Bob recognizes it as a strategic moment. In actuality, the landlord is saying she's now willing to make a particular move, namely letting him speak to her attorneys. Look how Bob uses this strategic moment to de-escalate the confrontation:

"You suggested turning the matter over to your attorneys. I think that's a good idea. Why don't you have one of your lawyers call me, and we'll review the contract together. I'm sure we'll be able to settle the matter."

This catches the landlord off guard. When she mentions attorneys, usually people are scared and back down. This guy Bob is *inviting* attorneys to get involved. She replies: "Uh—okay."

You may be wondering, "Why is her suggestion to involve her attorneys a strategic moment for Bob?" Two reasons:

- First, Bob isn't getting anywhere dealing with the

landlord. She believes she's right, and that perception of hers makes her unwilling to compromise. Bob doesn't know what to do, and she's suggesting he talk with someone else. Not a bad idea. Sure, the lawyer could turn out to be just as hard-nosed, but then again, the lawyer might be more reasonable. Bob figures it's worth a try.

- Here's the second reason the landlord's invitation is a strategic moment for Bob: She is offering to spend $150 per hour talking with him. That's how much her attorney costs. Every *minute* Bob spends with the lawyer, his adversary pays $2.50. Bob, on the other hand, pays nothing. Talk about having time on your side! After five hours, the attorney's fees will be so great, they'll equal one month's rent, and the landlord will have gained nothing.

Of course, she'll realize that. She'll see that Bob is calling her bluff and that she can't use her attorney to intimidate him into giving in. With that option gone, she may be more willing to negotiate.

The Rubber-Band Effect

There is one problem with seizing the moment. You risk what I call the Rubber-Band Effect. You know what happens when you stretch a rubber band: it snaps back. Human beings behave in a similar way. When they sense they've stretched too far, they tend to snap back, often to their original position. People back away not only because they get scared but also because they get realistic. They see the implications of what they've agreed to do and they itch to renege.

You can try to prevent the Rubber-Band Effect by proceeding slowly and checking with the other person: "Are you really comfortable agreeing to this? Do you want time to think it over?" However, sometimes it's wiser to accept their commitment and hope they fulfill it. If you test to see how secure it is, you risk losing it.

Case in point: The first day the new boss arrived at our company, he was drunk with excitement. He was saying "Yes!" to everything. "Yes!" to new employees. "Yes!" to complex legal documents. I poked my head in his office and asked, "Excuse me, sir, could I use a company car to commute to work?"

"Yes!" he said.

I did not want to press my luck and ask, "Uh, sir...are you *sure?*" I figured, if the boss ever wanted the car back, I'd return it. (PS. I did return the car when I left the company.)

In a business deal, you can often reduce the risk of the Rubber-Band Effect by insisting in advance on contract penalties. The idea is that the other person is less likely to renege if they'd have to pay a high price to do so. One example of a contract penalty is collateral on a loan. If you renege on your word, you pay a stiff penalty: the bank gets your collateral.

Another way to discourage the Rubber-Band Effect is to warn the other side that if they back out, so will you. If they want you to keep your word, presumably they'll think twice before breaking theirs.

But what if, despite all your efforts, the Rubber-Band Effect occurs, anyway? What can you do if the person's immediate limit suddenly shrinks and they're no longer willing to make the move you want?

Suggest a fallback move. A fallback move is smaller, easier to make, and less risky: it involves less change.

One of my students, Nancy, wanted paid time off because she was pregnant. She talked to the personnel director, and he promised to establish a formal policy.

The next day, he phoned Nancy to say he had changed his mind. He said an employee might want time off when the company couldn't afford it.

Fortunately, Nancy had a fallback. If the personnel director could not establish a formal policy covering everyone, would he agree to an informal arrangement just for her? He did. That move was much easier for him to make.

As this case illustrates, you should expect to go "two steps forward, one step back." You'll get close, you'll back away. Sometimes many times. And you must be prepared to adapt.

A salesman named Jack told me how he adapted: "My biggest customer, HP, was about to renew their contract with us. Then a competitor gave them a bid that was 20% lower than ours, and suddenly there was no way we were going to get that contract.

"Fortunately, I had a fallback move for HP to make. I told them, 'You know our track record; you don't know how the other guys will perform. If you give an

unknown firm *all* your business, and they don't perform, you'll be stuck.'

"'So how about this: let us match their price for the
first year, and give us 20% of the business. For you, it's
a no-risk insurance policy. You'll have someone to
depend on if the other guys can't deliver.'"

And here Jack smiled. "I knew nobody could make
a profit undercutting us 20% without sacrificing service. When the competition performed poorly, we were
in position to recapture the contract at our original
price."

Don't try to be brilliant

Jack's game plan was not very complex. Yet, we often
assume our strategy must be sophisticated. Time and
again, people ask me how they can develop a strategy
that is clever.

This question misses the point. Your aim is not to
be brilliant. It is not to create an intellectual work of
art that will be admired for its intricacies.

Your aim is to develop a plan that works.

There's a scene in *Raiders of the Lost Ark* where the
hero, Indiana Jones, is surprised by a master swords-
man who slices his blade brilliantly through the air.
This looks mighty scary until Indiana Jones pulls out a
gun and blows him away.

Moral: Don't try to be sophisticated.

Be *effective.*

Some of the most effective strategies are common-
place and unimpressive. Like crying to get attention.

Or proposing that you split the difference. Or agreeing that "first we'll do what you want, then we'll do what I want."

When the solution is so ordinary, many people conclude it was obvious all along. But it can take a lot of skill to find a strategy that suits your specific problem.

When my car horn was broken, I thought of lots of ideas. A new horn. A new fuse. A new connector tab. However, all those answers happened to be wrong. I took the car to my mechanic, and do you know what he did?

He soldered a broken wire. I had overlooked the one simple solution that would work. The cost: $25.50. "50 cents," he told me, "is for the solder. $25 is for figuring out that soldering was the right thing to do."

FIGURING OUT THE RIGHT THING TO DO is especially challenging when you're in the midst of a confrontation. That's when the four strategic steps are especially helpful.

How can you become so adept at strategic communication that you can use it to think on your feet?

❖❖ *Key points for applying ideas in:*
Strategic questions and answers

1. When deciding whether to reveal information, remember that revealing or concealing does not in-

herently give you power. Making the right decision
about what to reveal gives you power. Before revealing information, predict the other person's response.

2. As a general rule, go ahead and make the first offer
    *if your offer violates their expectations and is still
    within their immediate limit.* (For example, see
    page 205.)

3. To determine how much to request, learn the other
    person's perceptions about the bargaining process.
    • If the person has a bargainer's mindset, go in
       asking for *more* than their immediate limit will
       allow.
    • If they have the "honesty" mentality, make sure
       your request is *within* their immediate limit.

4. Before resorting to the strategy of making them
    suffer, recall the many reasons that this approach
    often fails. The other person perceives...
    • "This punishment is no worse than I had ex-
       pected."
    • "I can live with it."
    • "I'm so committed to my beliefs, I won't surren-
       der no matter what."
    • "I will not be humiliated."
    • "I'd set a precedent by caving in to pressure."
    • "I'm going to teach *you* a lesson."

5. Don't be afraid to take a stand against the other
    person *when it is strategically wise.* Contrary to the
    "win-win" philosophy, taking a tough stand *can*

settle an issue—and cooperating *can* continue the conflict.

6. Watch out for the Rubber-Band Effect—a sudden shrinkage in the other person's immediate limit. If they are no longer willing to make the move you want, suggest a fallback move.

7. Whenever they keep pushing, and you get annoyed, be patient: testing by pushing is a natural part of resolving problems. Often, they need to see that they've gotten the most possible, before they will be prepared to agree to a settlement.

Thinking on your feet

You now know how the four strategic steps work individually. Next observe how people use them together, to plan and think on their feet. Here are transcripts of actual conversations, along with tips to hone your strategic skills.

Books can get people a bit excited.

After reading a book on jogging, you may feel like lacing up your athletic shoes right away and running a marathon. After reading about strategic communication, you may feel like applying it right away on the spur of the moment during a confrontation.

In both cases, it's wise to practice first.

You may already be experienced at using many of the concepts in strategic communication. Successful people apply them intuitively. But you must become familiar specifically with using the four strategic steps, before you can expect to apply them adeptly under pressure.

What's the best way to get immediately comfortable with the four strategic steps and build your skill with them, so you can use them to think on your feet?

Begin with a low-risk problem

Don't use the method of strategic communication on your toughest dilemmas right away. Like that new pair of jogging shoes, a new method needs to be broken in. As you use it more and more, you become accustomed to it.

So begin practicing strategic communication on problems where the stakes are low and you don't care much about the outcome. As you become increasingly comfortable using the four strategic steps, you can apply them to increasingly difficult challenges.

Strategize when you're not under pressure

It is easy to get frustrated and overwhelmed if initially you use a new skill in a stressful situation. So at first, don't try to develop your next move in the heat of the moment when you're face-to-face with the other person.

Plan before the interaction. That's not only a good way to get accustomed to using strategic communication, it's also a wise rule of thumb no matter how experienced you are.

For example, let's say that for the last six weeks there has been a big project to get done at the office and the boss has asked you to work weekends at no extra pay. You're starting to feel taken advantage of, but what can you do about it?

1. *Decide whether you have a misunderstanding or a true disagreement.*
   "Would the problem go away if only my boss understood that I hate working weekends? Ha! She understands; she wants me to work weekends, anyway. A true disagreement."

2. *Create the other person's next move.*
   "What's the most I can get the boss to do right now? If I ask for overtime pay, she'll say she can't afford it. What's a smaller move she could make? She might agree to give me compensatory time off in exchange for my working weekends. That might be realistic."

3. *Use their own perceptions to convince them.*
   "What is the boss thinking? What are her per-

ceptions—and which ones should I build on? She thinks that we've all got to have a 'team attitude' and that the work needs to get done, no matter what. She'll be more receptive to me if she knows I will act in support of her beliefs, instead of trying to avoid overtime. I could begin by telling her: 'I know we've all got to pull together—and if that means working weekends, then we've got to do that.' Then I can go on to make my request, and she'll know I'm not trying to shirk my responsibilities."

4. *Predict the other person's response.*

"How will she respond? She might object that she can't give me time off if I've got a lot of work to do. So maybe I need to modify my request. Maybe I should ask her for compensatory time off *after the crisis passes and I'm caught up on my work.*"

You can strategize not only before the meeting but also during a break in the discussion. Whenever you find yourself getting stuck, call time out and review the four strategic steps to generate fresh ideas.

Review the conversation afterwards

The old saying goes, "You learn from experience," but that's not always true. Human nature, in the words of another cliché, is to "put the problem behind you" and never think of it again. Consequently, many people do the same dumb things over and over and never learn.

Just having experience does not mean you learn

from it. To learn from experience, you've got to reflect on what happened:

"What was I trying to accomplish?"

"What did I accomplish?"

"Why didn't things go as planned?"

"How can I improve next time?"

To get better at strategic communication, replay the conversation in your mind and see how you applied or failed to apply the four strategic steps. What move were you trying to get the other person to make? Did you understand their perceptions? The more you train yourself to think strategically, the more easily you'll be able to do it under pressure.

Observe other people's interactions

You can also sharpen your strategic skills by observing other people's interactions. Watch how each person follows or fails to follow one of the four strategic steps, and look what happens in the conversation as a result.

You can observe any conversation, whether it takes place at home or at the office, in person or on the phone—or even in a novel or on TV.

Let's take a typical workplace example, a conflict between two department heads—one from Manufacturing Engineering, the other from Production. Employees from the two departments have formed the Quality Team to suggest ways of producing better products, with advice from a consultant. The two department heads were supposed to oversee the Quality Team together; however, the consultant has sent all her invoices to Roger, the Production boss, and he's been so busy he's signed every one, without talking with Dawn, the manager of Manufacturing Engineering.

Today, Roger suddenly remembered that he and Dawn have to submit their first quarterly report on the team's progress to the division manager in three days. Roger began adding up the consultant's invoices.

The total was $15,000 over budget.

Roger has called Dawn into his office to discuss how they're going to write the report. (My strategic observations are in italics.)

Roger: We've got a big problem with the cost overrun, and I think the main thing is we've got to stick together, since we each bear responsibility.

Note the move he wants Dawn to make: he wants her to share the blame. But this move may not be realistic.

Dawn: Well, Roger, we may have had joint responsibility officially, but in reality I'm not to blame for this overrun. This is your overrun. You're going to have to explain it, not me. How do you plan to explain it?

Roger: I'm sure we can come up with something.

Roger wants to avoid a confrontation; that's why he chooses not to argue about who is to blame. Instead, he stays focused on asking her to help create an explanation.

There is one problem with this strategy. Why should Dawn help him if she perceives she bears no responsibility? That is a powerful perception, and Roger needs to address it effectively before she will cooperate.

Remarkably, he never does. He is so worried about preserving harmony that he tries to avoid discussing Dawn's perception. But it will not go away. Ignoring it is one of Roger's biggest strategic errors in the entire meeting.

Dawn: "We" are not to blame, Roger. You are to blame. I have a track record of financial responsibility. Apparently you run your department a bit differently. I, however, have a concern about my integrity.

Roger: Well, Dawn, your integrity is your concern, not mine. You cannot expect me to be responsible for your integrity.

Roger is steamed at Dawn's attacks, and his emotions are taking over. He is playing Tit-for-Tat, striking back. He is hardly in a strategic mode. He fails to predict her response to his jab. It sends the discussion spiraling downhill.

Dawn: Look, I'm not the one who signed off on all those invoices. You did it, not me. You did it, so you explain it.

Roger: You and I both have to explain it. You had joint responsibility. You are in this with me.

Dawn: Oh, no you don't! No way. I'm not going to take the blame for this. I'm not the one who ran this project over budget. And if there's an uproar about this, it's going to be a lot worse for you than for me. You're going to be the one with egg on your face.

Now they're pointing fingers at each other. The conversation has lost any constructive purpose. Fortunately, Roger recognizes this and refocuses the discussion.

Roger: Uh, look. You're talking about a lose-lose outcome here. I want to go for a win-win. Let's focus on our common commitment to improve quality. We still share that, right?

Dawn: Of course!

Roger: You're satisfied with the progress that the team has made?

Dawn: Absolutely! We've come up with some great ideas for improving quality.

Roger has gotten her to make one constructive move after another. First, she has acknowledged that she is committed to the team's goal; second, she has confirmed that she is satisfied with the team's progress.

Roger: Well, if the division boss focuses on this cost overrun, the team's going to be scrapped and we're both going to lose. All those great ideas will never get implemented.

Dawn: So what do you want me to do?

Now that Dawn has made a couple small moves, she is ready to go further. Fortunately, Roger is prepared with another move for her to make.

Roger: I want you to write a report with me in the next three days about what a good job the team is doing. We'll summarize all of the team's ideas for improving quality. You're willing to do that, right?

Dawn: Sure. It's short notice, but I'm willing.

Roger: And we'll say the program is so good that it deserves to continue despite the cost overrun.

Roger is asking Dawn to say, "The team has gotten so much accomplished, it should continue, even though we had the overrun." But as you'll see, Dawn misunderstands and thinks he wants her to say something different: "The program is so good, the cost overrun is justified."

Dawn: Oh, no you don't! There you go again.

The overrun is your responsibility. You've got to explain it, not me. How are you going to explain the cost overrun?

Roger: Well, how would *you* suggest we do it?

Dawn: No, no, that's *your* problem, not mine.

Roger: No, it's *our* problem, because if *we* don't stand together, the team is going to be scrapped.

Dawn: Well, *you* approved the cost overruns; now you've got to take the heat for them.

Dawn has now given several conversational cues that she is not willing to justify the cost overrun. Sharing the blame is clearly beyond her immediate limit.

But Roger is no longer asking her to share the blame. He has given up on that. Now he wants her simply to justify the continuation of the team based on its accomplishments. Unfortunately, he has failed to tell Dawn explicitly that his goals have changed, so she thinks he still wants her to share the blame.

If only Dawn understood his true request, she would say yes. Her sole concern is to avoid the blame. Unfortunately, Roger doesn't recognize that they have a misunderstanding about his request. He assumes that they have a true disagreement. And his solution is to give in.

Roger: OK. Let's say I take the heat in this report and say that I was so focused on other projects that I kept signing off on these invoices. You'd be willing to say that the team has made great progress, it's been worth the money, and the team is worth continuing?

Dawn: Yeah.

Dawn's simple strategy has finally paid off. Her strategy

has been to repeat her perception that he is to blame and to assert her immediate limit, to get him to make the move of accepting responsibility. Now, he has made that move.

Roger: And if I take the blame, you'd be willing to support the team enthusiastically?

Dawn: Absolutely! I support the team. I'm just worried about my reputation.

Roger: Then that's what we'll do. I think that if we both tell the division manager that the team is making great progress, the cost overrun will be no big deal.

Perhaps, but Roger did not have to take the full blame. He still could have gotten Dawn to co-author the report. If she perceived that her reputation was at risk, he could have suggested that their report focus solely on the team's progress, not on finances. Or that the report discuss plans to prevent future overruns, without finding fault.

Roger failed to develop fallback moves such as these for Dawn to make. Thus, when she balked at sharing the blame, he saw no option but to give in completely and shoulder the full blame himself.

By observing conversations through the lens of strategic communication, you'll become adept at spotting strategic errors and opportunities. You'll also see how successful people use the four strategic steps instinctively in the midst of an argument.

Focus initially on the first strategic step

After you've honed your skills with strategic communication by developing your next move when you're not under pressure, by critiquing other people's conversations and by reviewing some of your own in light of the four strategic steps, then—and only then—are you ready to test your skills on the spur of the moment.

The first time you use strategic communication to think on your feet, you may try to apply all the steps simultaneously. Typically, that's a mistake. You get overwhelmed and confused trying to focus on too many new ideas at once.

Instead, get comfortable with strategic communication one step at a time.

Focus initially on the first strategic step about distinguishing a misunderstanding from a true disagreement. At first, go into the discussion telling yourself, "No matter how emotional things get, I'm going to keep asking myself, *'Would the problem disappear if we understood each other better?'*" Once you train yourself to focus on the first strategic step automatically, you can start adding the second step, then the third, and so on.

By the way, during an argument, don't worry about reviewing the four strategic steps in order. You can cycle through them in any sequence that occurs to you.

And don't worry about trying to review all four strategic steps every time you say something. There is not enough time. Rather, think of each step periodically throughout the conversation.

Think of each strategic step as a question

Some students have found it helpful to recast all four strategic steps as questions they can ask themselves during the discussion.

1. Decide whether you have a misunderstanding or a true disagreement. *"Would the problem disappear if we understood each other better?"*
2. Create the other person's next move. *"What's the most I can get them to do right now?"*
3. Use their own perceptions to convince them. *"What are they thinking—and how can I build on it?"*
4. Predict the other person's response. *"How will this person respond?"*

Note that the third question *("What are they thinking—and how can I build on it?")* implies that you should focus on the person's immediate thoughts—instead of examining their deeper, underlying perceptions and selecting which perception to build upon.

This is because, initially, focusing on their immediate thoughts is much easier. Once you train yourself to become aware of the other person's immediate thinking, then you can focus on their underlying perceptions and ask yourself the more thorough question: *"What are their perceptions—and which ones should I build on?"*

Example of thinking on your feet

I'll show you how the mayor of a big city, Evelyn Sanders, used strategic communication to defuse what could have been a major confrontation with a developer, James Burns & Associates. (I've changed the names to protect confidentiality.) The mayor had hired Burns to run the city's golf course and build a confer-

ence center nearby. But then one day, a dramatic story appeared on the front page of the morning newspaper:

City Money Allegedly Used
for Trips to Bahamas

The city auditor has completed a confidential report showing that James Burns & Associates, the developer managing the municipal golf course, has spent $47,000 of golf-course earnings on questionable expenses, such as unexplained trips to the Bahamas.

Burns & Associates also has a city contract to build a conference center next to the golf course, and the report reveals that Burns has not only missed construction deadlines but also owes the city $100,000 in lease payments for that project.

A Burns spokesman said the firm had not seen the city auditor's report and could not comment.

Hours after the story appeared, several council members announced that at that evening's council meeting, they would try to cancel Burns' contracts for both the golf course and the conference center. Mayor Sanders' chief rival on the council blamed her for the mess, since she had hired Burns.

It was amidst this uproar that the mayor went into a meeting with Burns to decide how to deal with the brouhaha. I advised the mayor on this negotiation, and I debriefed her afterwards. I've noted in brackets what she was thinking each time she spoke, so you can see how she applied strategic communication throughout the discussion.

You'll see how the mayor distinguishes a misunder-

standing from a true disagreement, identifies Burns'
perceptions, and predicts his responses. Above all, she
creates one realistic move after another for him to
make.

She walks into the meeting with a clear goal: she
wants Burns to put $47,000 into an escrow account
and to submit to an independent audit. The city and
Burns will split the cost of the audit. If the audit finds
that Burns did nothing wrong, he'll get his full
$47,000 back. If he does owe anything, the city will
collect from the escrow account.

Mayor Sanders thinks that Burns will say yes to this
arrangement, because she is sure it will instantly defuse
the public criticism of both of them. How can anyone
complain about his squandering public money, if he's
handing over all the money in dispute?

But when the meeting begins, Burns is in no mood
to be conciliatory.

Burns: "You've got one heck of a way of communicating—spreading lies in the newspaper! What's the
idea? Are you trying to ruin my reputation?"

Mayor *[Burns misunderstands completely. He thinks
I'm out to get him. I want him to make a move, all right:
I want him to see that he's wrong. So I'm going to clear up
this misunderstanding of his.]:*

"Easy, Jim. I'm under fire, too, because of this
story. I wouldn't have leaked it. I wasn't the source."

Burns: "OK, well...I'm sorry. I know that your
neck is on the line, too. Your city auditor just doesn't
understand what it takes to run a golf course. We've

got to sit down and talk things out. You'll see we have not squandered $47,000."

Mayor *[Burns thinks that he can explain the whole problem away. So, what's the next move I want him to make? I want him to recognize that he can't resolve this issue merely by explaining himself.]:*

"I agree that the auditor may misunderstand, but, Burns, our problem today is *more* than a misunderstanding. You can't resolve it by clarifying communication, because you don't have time to clarify anything. The council is ready to cancel your contracts tonight. *Tonight!* The immediate problem is that we've got to restore the council's faith in you right now, you see?"

Burns: "No, no, no. We need time to work out this $47,000 issue. Why don't you ask the council to delay discussing my lease until you and I have a chance to resolve the $47,000?"

Mayor *[He wants me to give him time to talk things out, and I can't. That's beyond my immediate limit. The next move I want him to make is to recognize this reality.]:*

"There is no way the council will give you more time. No way. Impossible. They are so upset by that newspaper article, they intend to take action tonight."

Burns: "Well, your auditor is wrong. And we'd like the chance to prove it. We'd like to pay an independent auditor to investigate the $47,000 question. We'll pay whatever the auditor says we owe. But the city's construction deadlines on the conference center are unrealistic. We need to develop a realistic schedule with you. We need more time to build that center."

Mayor *[So he's volunteering to pay for an independent auditor himself! I hadn't even planned on suggesting that.*

If he's willing to make that big a move so early in our meeting, maybe I can get him to go a step further and agree to the escrow idea. To entice him, I'm going to build on his perception that he needs time to explain himself.]:

"Well, you do need a chance to explain yourself, and there's no time before tonight's council meeting. But I have an idea to convince them not to cancel your contracts tonight, so you have a chance to present your case. How about if you pay $47,000 into an escrow account pending the result of the independent audit. This way, we do not assume that you are at fault, but your payment will restore the council's confidence in you. Then they'll give you a chance to explain."

Burns: "$47,000 is a lot to put up all at once."

Mayor *[No, it's not. But how can I get Burns to see that? By drawing upon an overriding perception of his— that he can't afford to lose his city contracts.]:*

"$47,000 is paltry compared to the $2 million you'll lose if the council cancels your contracts for the golf course and the conference center."

Burns: "My Lord, you guys are going to bankrupt me! You can't do that to me!"

Mayor *[Uh-oh, he thinks I'm threatening him, his temper is boiling, and we're close to an argument. What move do I want him to make? I want him to back off. So I've got to convince him I'm not attacking him. Deep down, he knows that I want to solve the problem just as he does. I'll build on that perception.]:*

"Jim, I'm on your side. I'm not out blasting you. I'm working with you to find a way out of this mess."

Burns: "Well, if you cut us off on the conference center, it will take you at least a year to find another contractor. And in that year, you won't be able to book conferences. By your own estimates, you're going to lose....let's see here...*$3 million* in revenue! You're going to lose even more than we will!"

Mayor: "Yeah, but that's revenue, not— *[Whoa. I'm getting hooked. If I refute his point about who's going to lose more, he's going to respond by arguing with me.*

There's no point in arguing about who is going to lose more. I want him to refocus on what he can do to avoid losing anything. I want him to make the move of putting the $47,000 in escrow.] ...Uh, that's true. You're right. I want to save my $3 million, and I know you want to save your $2 million. That's why we need to work this out. Let's get a sense of perspective: $47,000 is like 2% of $2 million...right? If you put that $47,000 in escrow, you save the deal for both of us."

Burns: "Look, be reasonable. $47,000 is a heck of a lot. We're in this together, so I need you to talk straight. How much cash do I have to put into escrow for you to get the city council to stop harassing me?"

Mayor *[He's trying to get me to reveal my bottom line. I'd be willing to accept half of the $47,000 in escrow, but I'm not telling him that. Not while there's a chance that he'll put up the full $47,000. I really want the full $47,000. Then I know that the problem will be solved and the newspaper will stop hounding me. So I'll try to* *dodge his question about my bottom line. I want him to get distracted on a side issue.]:*

"You know, one thing the city council is concerned about is your expertise. This is the first golf course you've managed. They think maybe you need to hire some consultants."

Burns: "How dare they question my competency! They don't know anything about golf courses! You tell them to mind their own business!"

Mayor: "Actually, it *is* their business because... *[I'm getting sucked in again. He's going to respond by arguing with me. I need to stay focused. My goal is for him to say yes to the escrow arrangement. He believes the council is doubting his integrity. I'm going to build on that perception.]* OK, listen, we can get the council off your back. They are doubting you. They need to be reassured. If you put the money in escrow, they'll be reassured. You'll take the wind out of the sails of even your harshest critic. How can anyone be mad at you when you're putting up all the money that's in dispute?"

Burns: "Yes, I can see that. I think you're right."

Mayor *[This is a critical conversational cue. He is confirming that he concurs with my analysis. I have convinced him he needs to put up serious money. This is a strategic moment. Because he concurs with my analysis, I am probably going to be able to get the full $47,000.]:*

(Mayor Sanders remains silent.)

Burns: "I mean, I see your point, but...$47,000 is a lot of money. We could put up $30,000 or even $35,000. Would that make sense to you?"

Mayor [*Great! He's forgotten about pressing me for my bottom line. He is making me an offer—and even as he's making it, he's slipping higher, from $30,000 up to $35,000. That's an obvious conversational cue that he doesn't consider his own offer of $30,000 to be very serious.*

I'm going to see if I can convince him to go all the way to $47,000. I'm going to draw upon his overriding perception that he must restore his reputation.]:

"No, I don't think that $35,000 would make much sense. The auditor has accused you of doing away with $47,000. If you put up less than that, the council may suspect that your commitment to the city is less than 100%. We don't want them to doubt you. Putting the full amount in escrow today is the single best thing you can do to restore your reputation in the eyes of the council and in the general public immediately."

Burns: "Well, it is hard for us to put up money for something we didn't do. That's admitting fault. If we put up $47,000, and if the audit shows that we did nothing wrong, the $47,000 should be applied toward the $100,000 we owe in lease payments."

Mayor [*Amazing. Burns puts forward a good objection to the escrow arrangement—that putting money in escrow would be admitting fault—but then he undercuts his own objection by offering a solution to it! And the solution he offers is for him to give another concession—applying the $47,000 toward the lease debt! I haven't even asked for this additional concession.*

I've gotten more than I want from Burns. I won't push for even more; I'll simply get him to confirm everything.]:

"So we're in agreement. You'll make a good faith payment of $47,000 so we can proceed on the conference center. And if you are cleared by the independent audit, then the $47,000 will be applied to the $100,000 in lease payments. Right?"

Burns: "That's right. We want to restore the council's faith in us. And we want to convince them to give us more time to build the conference center."

Mayor *[If Burns wants "more time," he should have proposed specific changes to the construction schedule. And he should have made his $47,000 payment conditioned on those changes. Now that he's promised to pay the $47,000, I can afford to ignore the schedule issue.]:*

"Well, if you tell the city council that you've paid $47,000 in escrow in good faith, then I can certainly persuade them to go ahead on the conference center."

It may seem from this transcript that the mayor's thinking was ploddingly slow. On the contrary, it took her fractions of a second for her to think before she spoke. She was so experienced with strategic communication, to her it was instinctive.

Thus, she was able to recognize not only his mistakes but also her own—and fast enough to do something about them.

You're going to make mistakes. The important thing is to be aware of them when you make them so you can correct your course of action while you still have the chance. With strategic communication you have a compass to show you when you're going off track and to guide you back on course.

Thinking strategically becomes automatic

The more you use the four strategic steps, the more they will become second nature. By the end of a semester, students of mine have found themselves automatically cycling through the steps on the spur of the moment.

That's not to say every problem becomes easy to solve. But after reading this book, you now have an approach for solving it.

Strategic communication lends a structure to the complex process of deciding your next move. When you're having trouble figuring out what to do, you can depend on the four strategic steps. (Of course, you can also use strategic communication from the outset, to avoid trouble.) Strategic communication helps you break apart a complicated problem into manageable pieces, so you don't feel as overwhelmed.

The four strategic steps will help you prepare thoroughly, so you can walk in to a meeting with confidence. They will help you stay focused under pressure.

They will spare you from countless conversations where talking more only makes things worse.

❖ Key points for applying ideas in:
Thinking on your feet

1. Begin using strategic communication on a low-risk problem. As you become increasingly comfortable using the four strategic steps, you can apply them to increasingly difficult challenges.

2. Strategize when you're not under pressure. At first, don't try to develop your next move in the heat of the moment when you're face-to-face with the other person. Plan before the interaction.

3. Review the conversation afterwards to improve at strategic communication. Replay the conversation in your mind and see how you applied or failed to apply the four strategic steps.

4. Observe other people's interactions to further hone your tactical skills. Look at how each person in the discussion follows or fails to follow one of the strategic steps, and look at what happens in the conversation as a result.

5. Focus initially on the first strategic step. The first time you use strategic communication to think on your feet, don't try to apply all the strategic steps simultaneously. Begin by using one step at a time.

6. Think of each strategic step as a question that you can ask yourself when you are in the midst of a confrontation:

   - Decide whether you have a misunderstanding or a true disagreement. *"Would the problem disappear if we understood each other better?"*
   - Create the other person's next move. *"What's the most I can get them to do right now?"*
   - Use their own perceptions to convince them. *"What are they thinking—and how can I build on it?"*
   - Predict the other person's response. *"How will this person respond?"*

REFERENCE TOOLS

The Four Steps of Strategic Communication

1. **Decide whether you have a misunderstanding or a true disagreement.**

   "Would the problem disappear if we understood each other better?"

2. **Create the other person's next move.**

   "What's the most I can get them to do right now?"

3. **Use their own perceptions to convince them.**

   "What are they thinking— and how can I build on it?"

4. **Predict the other person's response.**

   "How will this person respond?"

Glossary and Index of Terms

The mentality that a first offer is a wish, a hope, never to be taken very seriously. The bargainer's mindset is: "You always bargain down a first offer."

The most that someone *ultimately* would be willing and able to do to satisfy you.

Signals that people send to indicate what they are prepared to do for you and when you are reaching their immediate limit.

A counterproductive pattern in which you say something, the other side replies, suddenly there's a stalemate, and nobody knows what went wrong. *Dances to deadlock* are always predictable.

A move that you will propose for the other person to make, should they fail to do what you *really* want. A fallback move is smaller, easier to make, and less risky: it involves less change.

A dance to deadlock in which you keep giving concessions in a futile attempt to appease the other person:

1. *You give concessions with nothing in return.*
2. *Those on the other side take your concessions.
   Then they decide whether you've given enough.
   No surprise, they ask for more.*
3. *You give more, to try to appease them.*
4. *They demand more, because for them this game is
   working well.*

A fundamental belief that many Americans rely upon:
*Deep down, we all agree. People just need to understand
each other better.* The assumption is: *There is no conflict, only poor understanding.*

The mindset that everyone should be open about what
they really want. When you make an offer, a person
with the "honesty" mentality assumes you are serious
about it, even if it is a first offer.

The most that the other person is willing and able to
do for you *right now.*

A failure to understand each other accurately.

Myth of the Miracle Meeting 56
The belief that when you get everyone together for a meeting, controversies large and small will vanish, thanks to the magic of understanding.

overriding perception 142
A perception of the other person's that is more persuasive to them than another perception of theirs that you wish to challenge. By drawing upon their overriding perception, you can succeed at convincing them.

Rubber-Band Effect... 213
The tendency of human beings (like rubber bands) to snap back, often to their original position, when they sense they've stretched too far.

Selfishness Syndrome 83
A syndrome in which you respond to the stress or emotional burden of a problem by becoming self-centered, disregarding the other person.

strategy..15
An approach to help you achieve your goal.

strategic communication......................................16
A method to help you develop a strategy for resolving a disagreement. Since there is no magic formula for resolving all issues, strategic communication offers four steps you can use to *create* a strategy for *your specific*

situation. The method is designed to steer you clear of common pitfalls in which communication backfires.

A dance to deadlock in which the frustration of talking in circles escalates into communication breakdown:

1. *I make a demand, you make a demand.*
2. *I explain my position, you explain yours.*
3. *I announce I'm digging in, you do the same.*
4. *I stop talking, you stop talking.*

The most direct method to gauge someone's immediate limit. You make a proposal or take a stand and see whether they budge. If they absolutely refuse, you know you've reached their immediate limit.

A pattern in which you treat the other person the way they treat you. If they're nice, you're nice; if they play hardball, you play hardball.

A failure to agree that would persist despite the most accurate understanding.

A conversational routine where, intentionally or not, you entice the person to take an opposing stand— which gives you the perfect excuse for attacking them:

1. You ask your opponents: "Will you give in?"
2. Regrettably, they refuse.
3. You claim they are stubborn—and attack!

A common approach for dealing with a difference of opinion: each person starts with the assumption that they are right; then they push their point of view, determined to get their way, convinced that they can get the other side to give in.

The credo that you should help the other person toward their goal and that they should reciprocate by helping you toward yours. In other words, you help each other achieve a "win."

Indexed Outline of the Book

THE SOLUTION:
THE FOUR STEPS OF STRATEGIC COMMUNICATION

Strategic step #1:
**Decide whether you have a misunderstanding
or a true disagreement** 41

Index of Tables

Index of David Horsey's Illustrations

Credits: The Abilene story is adapted from the writings and experience of Jerry B. Harvey, professor of management science at George Washington University. His books include *The Abilene Paradox* (1988 Lexington).
The preacher story is from Gumperz' *Discourse Strategies*, ©1982 Cambridge University Press. Reprinted with permission of Cambridge University Press. I've drawn from Walton & McKersie's *A Behavioral Theory of Labor Negotiations: An Analysis of a Social Interaction System* (Cornell University, 1991) and from Lustberg's *Winning When it Really Counts* (Simon & Schuster, 1988) and his video, by permission of Arch Lustberg Communications, Inc., Washington, DC. The video *Controlling the Confrontation: Arch Lustberg on Effective Communication Techniques* is distributed by ALA Video/Library Video Network, 1-800-441-8273.
Thanks to Dow Jones. (Reprinted by permission of the *Wall Street Journal.* ©1995 Dow Jones & Company Inc. All rights reserved worldwide.) And thanks to the *San Jose Mercury News*. (©1992 San Jose Mercury News. All rights reserved. Reproduced with permission.) *We Can Work It Out* is abridged (©1965 Maclean Music). The auction is discussed by Shubik (1971), Teger (1980), and Neale & Bazerman (1991).

ACKNOWLEDGMENTS

H ow can you resolve problems when talking makes things worse? Many people over the years have contributed to answering that question, developing, testing, and refining the method of resolving problems in this book. Special thanks to my University of California colleagues, Mike Stafford and Don Ray. Mike's camaraderie and love of debating sharpened ideas and examples throughout the book. He listened to my lectures and gave me incisive critiques. Don had a talent for catching me when I wasn't communicating clearly, which usually meant that I wasn't thinking clearly. Then, encouragingly, he helped me distill the concept that I was having trouble articulating.

Marilyn Sandifur meticulously pored over the book proposal and helped me fashion it word by word. Dorothy Wall expertly guided me to make sure that the result was commercially successful. Susan Page steered me clear of many pitfalls in publishing. She recommended Dorothy and also Patti Breitman, who became my agent. Patti put her heart into this project.

At Andrews and McMeel, I'm grateful to Linda Webster and Allan Stark for believing in this book and for never being too busy to offer support.

Alice and Rich Stiebel, Joe Macaluso, Fay Bauling, Hal Anjo, Joanna Robinson, Carew Papritz, Judith Robinson, Suzanne Hirsch, Jay Ginsberg, and Howard Smith read drafts of the book and gave me terrific comments. Alice is a top-flight English consultant;

she advised me on linguistic issues. She, Joanna, and Rich proofread the manuscript.

I was fortunate to have Claudia Marshall, whose writing I have long admired, as my editor. Her insights improved the dialogue, structure, chapter titles—in short, *everything.*

David Horsey created imaginative and humorous drawings that powerfully communicate themes in the book. His talent leaps off the page. Roy Minor lent his artistry and years of experience to the design of the text, tables, and jacket. He made everything easy to read and eye-catching. Brian Rhea's caring touch and keen eye sharpened the quality of the computer graphics and photographs.

Ivor Robinson has an incredible voice. He is the announcer for the book-on-tape. The post-production was done by Jay Ginsberg, a wizard at audio. Lou Lipcon and Fay Curtis, improvisational actors, skillfully re-created a negotiation for the book-on-tape.

For legal help, thanks to Mike Antonello, Nena Wong, Susan Schiff, Sally Talarico, Kevin Donovan, Allan Blau, Pam Friedman, Fran Toohey, and Carol Williams at the Authors Guild, which I encourage every author to join. (The Guild is in New York.)

My greatest debt for this book is to my witty wife Naomi, and not simply because she provided a rich supply of anecdotes. She kept critiquing drafts rigorously and patiently, even though she knew that each critique would result in yet another draft for her to review. This is love.

My Muse of storytelling is Fay Bauling. Also, her motto "face reality!" underlies the advice in this book to assess a situation realistically, not optimistically.

My father Rich inspired me with his talent for patiently isolating the underlying root of a problem instead of focusing on superficial symptoms. My mother Alice instilled in me a love of critical thinking, language, and psychology. I share these and many other interests with my brother Jonathan.

This book is dedicated to Naomi, Fay, Rich, Alice, and Jonathan.

Dr. David Stiebel...in person!

The internationally renowned negotiation adviser delivers keynote conference presentations on winning cooperation, building teams, and resolving conflict... *when talking makes things worse!*

Using live demonstrations, he gets the whole audience involved and provides original insights and new tools that attendees can apply right away on the job.

For information write:

Whitehall & Nolton, Publishers
5120 Northaven
Dallas, TX 75229-4353 USA

New! The Video Workshop
When Talking Makes Things *Worse!*

Now's your chance to apply the principles you've just learned.

See live interactions. Try to spot the strategic errors and opportunities yourself.

Then get incisive commentary from Dr. David Stiebel, the renowned negotiator who has used strategic communication to guide countless executives through disputes.

This interactive video workshop is an ideal tool for developing professional skills for your organization.

The video workshop is in production. To get details when it becomes available, send in the form below.

-------✂-----copy or clip this page and mail!----✉--------

Name _____ Address _____

City _____ State, Zip_____

When Talking Makes Things *Worse!* Video
Whitehall & Nolton, Publishers
5120 Northaven
Dallas, TX 75229-4353 USA

Did you borrow this book?

U sing this page, now you can get your own copy of **When Talking Makes Things** *Worse!* As you practice strategic communication, you'll need to refer to the four steps. That's why you should keep one copy of **When Talking Makes Things** *Worse!* at home and another copy at work.

Need a gift for a friend or colleague?

When Talking Makes Things *Worse!* makes an ideal present. The book is also available on audiocassette, to enjoy while driving or exercising.

(If you'd like copies for a group or department, quantity discounts are available.)

-------✂-----copy or clip this page and mail!----✉--------

Order Form. Send check for $29.95 each (price includes shipping). In TX, send $32.42 due to sales tax. *Specify:* ___ # of books and ___ # of books-on-tape. We'll send the book unless you specify the tape format.

Name _____Address _____

City _____State, Zip _____

Send to: Whitehall & Nolton, 5120 Northaven, Dallas, TX 75229. All sales are final. Allow 4-6 weeks delivery.